TONY STREATHER

Soldier and Mountaineer

1926 – 2018

The tale of a man who sought always to go
a little further, beyond that last blue
mountain barred with snow.

by

Robert Turner and Henry Edmundson

with best wishes

Robert Turner

Tony Streather, Soldier and Mountaineer
Copyright ©
(Henry Edmundson & Robert Turner 2021)

All rights reserved

No part of this book may be reproduced in any form by photocopying or any electronic or mechanical means, including information storage or retrieval systems, without permission in writing from both the copyright owners and the publisher of the book.

ISBN: 978-178456-780-4
Paperback

First published 2021 by Upfront Publishing
Peterborough, England.

An environmentally friendly book printed and bound in England
by www.printondemand-worldwide.com

*"We are the Pilgrims, master; we shall go
Always a little further; it may be
Beyond that last blue mountain barred with snow
Across that angry or that glimmering sea,*

*White on a throne or guarded in a cave
There lies a prophet who can understand
Why men were born: but surely we are brave,
Who take the Golden Road to Samarkand."*

James Elroy Flecker

Contents

Tony's Thanksgiving Service 7

The Boy from London Town 15

India, Pakistan and the Mountains 20

The Norwegian Expedition to Tirich Mir — 1950 31

K2, the Savage Mountain — 1953 40

Kangchenjunga, the Untrodden Peak — 1955 64

Haramosh — 1957 73

The Army Mountaineering Association 86

The Soldiering Life 93

Soldiers on Everest — 1976 114

A Soldier to the End 126

Two Presidents 132

Retirement 136

Acknowledgements 142

Tony's Thanksgiving Service

On Saturday 1st December 2018, the little church of St. John the Baptist at Hindon, Wiltshire, was packed with over two hundred friends and family in a space intended for a mere one hundred. The villagers had closed the road adjacent to the church for the duration of the service. Tony Streather's seven grandchildren — Will, Kate, Polly, Tom, Antony, George, and Ashley — took turns reading Rudyard Kipling's *If* and Bugler Augustine Dzakpasu from the Band of the Rifles sounded the Regimental Call of the Gloucestershire Regiment followed by the Last Post and the Reveille.[1] Many former members of the 'Glorious Glosters' surely shed a tear. Tony's ashes were buried alongside those of his beloved Sue, and, as Tony would have wished, the entire company retired to the Lamb, which was in sight of Apple Tree Cottage where Tony spent so many happy years amongst his friends.

During the service, Sir Chris Bonington spoke of Tony's climbing achievements:

"Although we never climbed together there was a strong synchronicity in our lives. We were both born in North London before the Second World War. We went to the same school, University College School, and had similar childhoods wandering on Hampstead Heath.

"In those days, all expeditions to the Himalayas needed a Transport-Liaison Officer, a role Tony readily volunteered for. But most liaison officers went no further than base camp — not so with Tony. He could not resist getting involved in the climb, working with and encouraging the high-altitude porters, joking with them in fluent Urdu, humping loads

---

[1] The Gloucestershire Regiment was a merger of the 28th (North Gloucestershire) Regiment of Foot dating from 1694 and the more recent 61st (South Gloucestershire) Regiment of Foot.

with them, very fit from his military duties chasing over high passes on the North-West Frontier. He discovered that he was a natural at high altitude, going stronger the higher he climbed, no doubt thanks to his uncommonly low resting heartbeat.

"Invited by the leader of the Norwegian 1950 expedition to Tirich Mir to join the summit team, he made the summit with no high-altitude gear, wearing army issue hobnail boots and pyjamas under his camouflage smock and trousers. On his return to Britain he was invited to join the Alpine Club, which Tony initially thought was merely some sort of gentlemen's club.

"A prospective candidate for the 1953 Everest Expedition, he went to the assessment on Mont Blanc and was found to be faster than any of the others on a straightforward snow plod but lacking any obvious technical experience. Hence, he was politely rejected. About the same time, a letter arrived from Charles Houston inviting him to join the American K2 expedition. This was as both Transport Officer and full climbing member of an otherwise all-American team — ironic considering that the South Col route to Everest is a snowbound route whilst the Americans were attempting the far harder and steeper mixed ground of the Abruzzi Spur on the most difficult of all the 8,000-metre peaks. The team of eight seasoned climbers did not include any high-altitude porters.

"All eight climbers reached the shoulder at 7,700 metres, only to sit out a savage storm for seven days. The general deterioration at that altitude caused member Art Gilkey to suffer a blood clot in his calf which spread to his lungs. Being unable to walk, he was wrapped in his sleeping bag and hauled down. Whilst crossing a slope of pure ice, with Gilkey belayed to an ice axe, one of the team fell and pulled down all but the last man, Pete Schoening. With lightning reaction, Schoening jammed his ice axe behind a boulder and held the entire party. Tony, with typical

understatement, commented that it really was an extremely tense situation. The rest is history. The next day Gilkey was nowhere to be seen, and the remaining climbers embarked on an epic descent off the mountain. The superb teamwork in response to adversity by an expedition that was years ahead of its time made a deep impression on Tony.

"Perhaps this was why Tony had no hesitation in accepting the invitation of Charles Evans to join his reconnaissance to Kangchenjunga in 1955. There were similarities with K2 — both Houston and Evans were medical men, and Tony felt an immediate empathy with Charles Evans describing him as a terrific leader with a dry, quiet sort of way about him.

"Later in an interview with Jim Curran, Tony recounted: 'We all became great chums and a close team … though of course I lacked the technical skill of Joe Brown. I often tried not to use oxygen because I found the extra weight of carrying the stuff offset any good it was doing me. I was selected for the second summit bid with Norman Hardie after Joe Brown and George Band. We went to the top camp, and the next day they returned triumphant but very tired as it was getting dark. They explained that at the very last there was a bit of climbing up a chimney. Until then Joe had found the whole thing a bore, plodding about in the snow, but now he had used a sling and hand jams. Joe said: 'Have a go, but you probably won't get up the final bit', because he knew that neither of us were great rock climbers.

'Well, off we went, and we had a drama on the way up. Norman who was leading had the misfortune of seeing one of his oxygen cylinders slip out of the carrying frame. I gave him one of mine and followed using the remaining one very sparingly, at about one litre a minute. Anyway, we got to the famous place that Joe talked about. We still had crampons on, didn't like the look of it, so just went round a bit and there was a nice little

snow ridge going straight to the top. It was a lovely, very clear day and we hung around just below the summit for some time. On the way down, the little oxygen I had ran out. Coming down was a very tedious business.'

"The first ascent of Kangchenjunga was a fantastic expedition and experience and I suspect that this is what influenced Tony when the Oxford University Mountaineering Club undergraduates invited him to join them on Haramosh in 1957, a magnificent and complex peak of 7,400 metres in the Karakoram. This would be just a recce, with Tony looking forward to helping the young climbers. Then comes more history. Bernard Jillott and John Emery were proceeding along a minor summit ridge, against Tony's advice, when an avalanche swept them 300 metres into a snow basin. They miraculously survived, but then ensued a desperate rescue attempt during which, despite Tony's heroic efforts and determination, two undergraduates perished and a third suffered terrible frostbite. There is no doubt that the Haramosh tragedy remained with Tony for the rest of his life.

"This was followed in 1959 by an expedition that saw the first ascent of Malubiting East, a 6,000-metre unclimbed peak in the Karakoram, and then in 1976 the Army Mountaineering Association expedition to Everest. Tony was expedition leader of this very well planned assault via the South Col. Henry Day, the climbing leader and Jon Fleming, the expedition organiser, described Tony as a superb leader. Quiet, unflappable, excellent at briefing his team, a good delegator of responsibility and a good listener involving his key people in the decision-making process.

"But there was tragedy at the beginning — the death of Terry Thompson who accidentally fell into a concealed crevasse at advance base. Tony handled it with his customary calm and common sense. Above the South Col, only the Army Mountaineering members were *involved. Four officers carried the gear and helped establish the top camp for two SAS corporals, Brummie Stokes and Bronco Lane. They made it to the summit, but the descent turned into another epic as bad weather forced a bivouac near the summit.*

"In 1992 Tony was elected President of the Alpine Club and is remembered by colleagues as superb at chairing meetings. Over many years he helped John Hunt's spirited endeavours to take disadvantaged youngsters to discover the great outdoors and help find themselves.

"Tony remains one of the very great trailblazers of that golden age of Himalayan climbing in the 1950s, who stumbled upon climbing as though by chance."

Robert Turner, his old friend from days serving with Tony in the Glosters, then spoke:

"Lt Col Harry Reginald Anthony Streather OBE, born on 24th March 1926 — known to all as Tony — was an extraordinary character who almost by accident 'tied on the rope of the man ahead' and began climbing mountains. Once he had tasted the call of the hills, he never regretted his lifetime's involvement with high places. Throughout his career, he encouraged others, especially young people, to follow in his footsteps.

"He helped found the Army Mountaineering Association. He was elected a member of the Alpine Club, though he had previously never climbed in the Alps and was subsequently elected the club's President during a difficult period when it sought to cast off its Victorian image and provide the home for aspiring young mountaineers.

"He persuaded the Army Council to recognise 'adventure training' as an official army activity and thus stop the practice of docking a soldier's pay and his pension entitlement if he was engaged in such activities. Initially, however, Tony was a victim of this official short-sightedness and

suffered financial penalties while taking part in his expeditions to the Himalayas. However, representations by the Colonel of his regiment resulted in him having his lost pension rights restored to him — though not without reluctance on the part of some Army chiefs. In a curious way, Tony had the last laugh. The Ministry of Defence would not simply backdate his pension entitlement, but instead insisted on him serving an equivalent extra period of service, which had the effect of entitling him to a larger pension thanks to a pay rise which occurred during this period.

Tony Streather at home in Baltistan, conversing with local boys in their dialect, ca. 1957.

Courtesy of the Streather family.

"He gained for Outward Bound pursuits the recognition in the Army that they deserved. He restored the reputation of the Army's Outward Bound School in Tywyn, North Wales. He planned and led expeditions on behalf of Sir John Hunt's Endeavour Training primarily for the

younger generation. His remarkable record on three of the highest mountains in the world is now well recognised.

"*His army career began in an unusual way. He was one of the last British officers to serve in the Irregular Frontier Forces of the legendary North-West Frontier Province, serving during the late 1940s and early 1950s with the Rajputana Rifles, the Zhob Militia, the Tochi Scouts and the Chitral Scouts. He recalled living and working with the Pathan tribesmen, patrolling the Afghan border, sometimes on horse and sometimes on camel but mainly on foot. The mountains were all around him — climbing steep ridges and crossing snow -covered passes up to 12,000 feet were just part of his daily routine. He saw first-hand in both India and Pakistan, especially as the ADC to the last British Governor of the North-West Frontier Province, the tragic consequences of the hurriedly planned partition of former British India.*

"*As a very young man he had a thousand men under his command. He had to seek out and buy the mounts needed by his Scouts. He became fluent in the languages and dialects of all with whom he served and thereby gained their trust and admiration. He even had to arrest and depose a local ruler — quite an achievement for a twenty-four-year-old.*

"*On his return to the UK in 1950, he joined the Gloucestershire Regiment, the 28th/61st Regiment of Foot, which became known as the 'Glorious Glosters' as a result of their heroic stand against overwhelming numbers of invading Chinese troops across the Imjin River in the Korean War. The bulk of the 1st Battalion were captured and spent two terrible years as POWs. Tony's first task on returning to the UK from Pakistan was to take charge of the first group of volunteers who set sail for Korea to rebuild the Regiment.*

"*He served in a succession of regimental appointments, eventually commanding the Battalion in Berlin and Northern Ireland. He served as* *an instructor at the Royal Military Academy at Sandhurst and at the Army School of Infantry at Warminster whence he was seconded to the Malaysian Jungle Warfare School to raise a new regiment skilled in jungle warfare for the Malaysian Army. He was subsequently seconded to the 6th Queen Elizabeth's Own Gurkha Rifles to fight in Borneo. Later he was to return to the Far East to revive and command a jungle warfare wing for the School of Infantry, which sadly he had also to close down after three very successful years training men from the Armies of the Commonwealth.*

"Although his Army service never had quite as colourful experiences as his six expeditions to the mountains, it remained the core of his life. On retiring from the Army, he became the Estates Manager at Sandhurst for ten very happy years.

"He married Sue (née Huggan) in 1956, having met her when she was maid of honour and he best man at the wedding of two of his closest friends, David and Felicity Metcalfe. Sue bravely endured his urge to keep returning to the mountains as she brought up their four children, Charlie, Peter, Phil and Sally. Tony was devastated when he lost Sue in 2005.

"Tony, a mountaineering legend in his own lifetime, seldom spoke of his personal life, save for two or three occasions during interviews and in a few articles which he wrote for the journals of the Alpine Club and the Army Mountaineering Association. He always made light of his achievements and the extraordinary events he lived through. His is a story that deserves the telling."

The Boy from London Town

Tony was the younger son of Reginald Streather, a successful North London Chartered Surveyor and builder, and his wife Gertrude, née Heygate.

Reginald Streather, born in 1899, and his older brother Edward born a year earlier both went to School House at Clifton College in Bristol. Edward joined the Royal Flying Corps but was killed on his very first flight in 1917. Reginald went to the Royal Military College at Sandhurst, as it was then known, and served as a Lieutenant in the Royal Horse Artillery between 1918 and 1919 and in the Second World War joined, as a Special Constable, the Mounted Branch of the Metropolitan Police.

Clifton was perhaps a surprising choice of school for a family from London, but it had gained a serious reputation as one of the foremost Victorian public schools based on the Rugby tradition. At that time Clifton boasted such heroes as Earl Douglas Haig, the Commander-in-Chief of the British Army in the First World War, and the Younghusband brothers, both of whom were involved in the classic North-West Frontier campaign of 1895 in which a small band of Indian troops was sent to relieve their fellow soldiers trapped in Fort Chitral. Interestingly, Chitral became part of Tony's own domain when he served on the North-West Frontier.

Tony's father, on leaving school and the Army, qualified in 1921 as a Chartered Surveyor and ran a successful building company in North London. He was Master of the Aldenham Harriers and Director of the Hendon Horse Show for many years. He also hunted with the Hertfordshire and encouraged in Tony a love of horses.

Tony and his younger brother, Robin, had been due to follow their father and uncle to Clifton, but at the start of the war in September 1939 the school wisely moved out of Bristol to Bude, and Tony instead went to University College School in North London. In one of those quirks of fate, it was also the school attended later by his friend and colleague in the world of Himalayan climbing, Sir Chris Bonington. Tony managed to pass the School Certificate but did not regard himself as a scholar. Nevertheless, he was Head Boy, Captain of Rugby and the RSM of the school's Officer Training Corps. From the age of sixteen, Tony also served in the Home Guard.

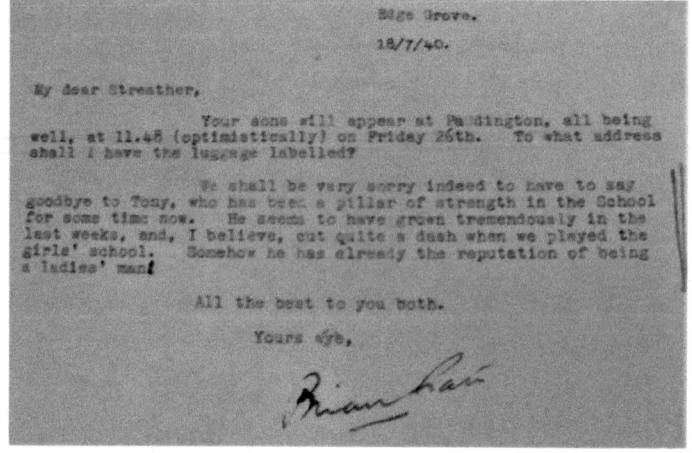

A ladies' man at the age of fourteen. Letter from the headmaster of Edge Grove school to Tony's father, on the occasion that Tony left Edge Grove for University College School in North London.

Courtesy of the Streather family.

Some time in 1944, a former Indian Army officer gave a lecture at his school on service life in India and clearly struck a chord. Thus, when Tony left school the same year and began his National Service, having been initially recruited into the Queen's Royal Regiment, he immediately sought to join the Indian Army. It was clear that the war in Europe was virtually at an end, but in the Far East the Japanese had still to be beaten, and the prospects for a young soldier there looked far more enticing. Surprisingly, the Indian Army was still recruiting young men to be trained as potential officers, even though independence was very much in the wind.

Tony Streather at the beginning of his military career, in the Queen's Royal Regiment, ca. 1944.

Courtesy of the Streather family.

He soon gained acceptance into the Indian Army and underwent some basic training at Maidstone — at the time of the V1 blitz — before catching a troopship for India. This was still a dangerous passage due to the presence of a few remaining German U-boats and the submarines of the Japanese Navy. After disembarking at Bombay, he continued by train to the Officer Training School at Mhow, in what is now Madhya Pradesh state, where the staff were surprised by the number of young potential officers still being sent to India.

He must have impressed his superiors at the training school because he gained a commission into the 1st Battalion of the prestigious Rajputana Rifles, then stationed in Baluchistan, the most westerly province of British India, bordered on the west by Iran and to the north-west by Afghanistan. He had sought to join the regiment as a result of a recommendation of a friend of his father, Harry Neale, who had served in the regiment. Tony was commissioned in early 1945 and was initially sent for jungle training which he completed just as the atom bombs were dropped on Japan. With the war in the Far East at an abrupt end, Tony returned to the regimental depot in Delhi and was then posted to Fort Sandeman, a particularly remote part of the tribal territories.

Few people other than the politicians were contemplating independence for India quite so hurriedly after the end of the war and consequently most were unprepared for the partition of the country into Muslim Pakistan and Hindu India. The Rajputana Rifles was still formed from a number of historic Regiments founded during the time of the Honourable East India Company. Hence, within the single Regiment, each religion was represented by a distinct Company. 'A' Company was formed of the martial race, the Rajputs, 'B' and 'C' companies were made up of Hindu Dogras, whilst 'D' Company were

Muslim. But all owed their allegiance to the Regiment rather than to their respective faiths. The Rajputana Rifles had served with great distinction in North Africa and Italy as part of the 4th Indian Division without any rancour or animosity between the various Companies.

India, Pakistan and the Mountains

Tony's six years in India and Pakistan coincided with the terrible events of the Partition of India, the consequences of which, such as the division of Kashmir, remain as political sores more than seventy years later. He served on the legendary North-West Frontier, living amongst the local tribes and learning their languages, dialects and customs which he never forgot. A delightful photograph shows him sitting on the ground by Kutwal Lake, during the expedition to Haramosh in the Karakoram in 1957, amiably chatting with a group of local boys. The boys would be speaking Urdu or their local dialect of Pushtu and must have been delighted to talk with this foreigner in their own tongue.

The Himalayas form the backbone of Asia, straddling the long frontier between Tibet in the north and India and Nepal to the south. But in the far north-west corner lie the equally imposing ranges of the Hindu Kush and Karakoram where during the late 19th century three world powers met almost head-on. The Tsarist Russian Empire had inexorably extended its suzerainty across central Asia, the Manchu Chinese were becoming increasingly influential in Tibet and further north, while the British Raj remained the undisputed power in the Indian subcontinent to the south. In the so-called Great Game, these players interminably jockeyed for position and influence.

Complicating this picture was neighbouring Afghanistan. Despite and perhaps because of the troubles they had suffered at the hands of the Afghans in a succession of wars, the British sought to establish a definite border with Afghanistan. Sir Henry Durand, an Indian civil servant, embarked on this task in 1893. In fact, two demarcations became necessary, the most westerly defining the so-called Tribal Territories that abutted Afghanistan directly, and to the east a second boundary which marked the eastern limit of the Tribal Territories and the beginnings of the Administrative Territory governed from Calcutta, and later from Delhi. The Tribal Territories were administered using local militias commanded by British officers, and this is where Tony spent most of his time. He thus took part in the very last days of the Great Game.

The North-West Frontier which became Tony's home for six years was harsh but exciting terrain in which to begin his thirty-six years of military service. The area was divided into Agencies, each with its local ruler and a Political Agent appointed by the central colonial administration. The Political Agent in effect governed the territory and was aided by Assistant Political Agents distributed in the main population areas. In each Agency, armed police called Scouts were notionally answerable to the local ruler but in effect constituted the law enforcement arm of the Political Agent. In all, there were about fifteen such Scout units distributed along the Tribal Territories. Each unit of Scouts took its name and its recruits from its specific locality.

The Scouts were an idea of George Nathaniel Curzon, who had visited the North-West Frontier as an MP in the 1890s and become Viceroy nine years later. He recommended that the regular Indian Army forces should be withdrawn into the main body of the Indian subcontinent, and that irregular Levies or Scouts be made responsible for maintaining law and order in the border regions.

Fort Sandeman was a typical frontier post, named after Sir Robert Groves Sandeman, a British Raj officer. It stood on a hill overlooking the flat plains of the Zhob River, on the road between Quetta and Peshawar. It provided the headquarters for the Zhob Scouts, but it also housed three regular battalions of the Indian Army which served there on rotation. The Fort remains intact today, preserved as a museum. Its distinctive tower, battlements and flagstaff stand alongside the Political Agent's Residence. Robert Sandeman's piano and all the 1930s-style furniture remain in the house.

Fort Sandeman in the 1930s, showing the military barracks on the plain.

When Tony was posted to Fort Sandeman with the Rajputana Rifles, his first assignment was as Signals Officer, but not with the sophistication of radios. Instead he had to rely on flag signals, heliographs and pigeons. Radios were just coming into use for a limited number of purposes. Other antiquated practices persisted. The Brigade moved in the old-fashioned manner by posting pickets on the tops of the cliffs on either side of its route with the precaution of mounting guards to the front and rear. It was a traditional way of manoeuvring large units through the savage and mountainous terrain. Tony, as a new young officer, must have found the conduct of operations in the regular army both ponderous and outdated, so he requested a secondment from his parent regiment to join the Zhob Scouts. His timing was fortunate. With Partition only months away, the bulk of the Rajputana Rifles were obliged to withdraw to the new Dominion of India. Tony thus remained in the North-West Frontier Province.

Tony in typical garb worn by officers of the North-West Frontier Scouts, with round-topped hat or pakol made of home-spun wool. Photograph was taken when Tony served in Chitral, his cap badge representing the Chitral Scouts horned ibex.

Courtesy of the Streather family.

The Zhob Scouts comprised up to a thousand or more men and served under the command of just two British officers. The Scouts had been raised by a cavalry officer, William Raikes-Hodson, in 1852 from Pashtun and Baluch tribesmen and derived from an even earlier band of locals recruited by Sir Henry Lawrence after the first Sikh War in 1846. As locals, the Scouts understood the local terrain and tribal customs intimately, and, most importantly, knew who could be trusted. The Scouts wore native garb — the smock and baggy trousers, with a round-topped hat or *pakol* made of homespun wool, and when necessary a sheepskin jerkin. The wool clothing was dyed khaki, originally using river mud! This drab colour well suited the rocky terrain in which they were deployed. The Officers wore the same dress. Each wore a regimental badge — in the case of the Chitral Scouts with whom Tony later served the badge displayed the horns of an ibex.

The Scouts were no easy option. Young officers seeking secondment had to undergo a rigorous selection procedure and needed to be fluent in the local dialect. Tony passed with flying colours. It was the life he had been dreaming about, with more opportunities and excitement than he could ever have experienced in a more formal regular Army unit.

Tony's first appointment was as Adjutant to the Commanding Officer of the Zhob Scouts, and being just twenty-one years old he sought to add a degree of *gravitas* to his appearance by growing a moustache, which remained with him for the rest of his life. His responsibilities were wide-ranging. Each Scout unit controlled vast areas of tribal country equipped with a number of forts which could house small contingents of militia. Under his command was a mounted troop of 183 horses and a pair of twenty-five-pounder field guns which were occasionally dragged out when a village was being raided by marauding Afghan tribes. The key was speed. The Scouts had to move easily across the rough and arid terrain. One daily exercise was particularly tense — the evening watering of the horses in rivers close to camp, easy prey to bandits eager to catch the troops off guard and make off with a few animals.

In the wider world, meanwhile, the date set by Lord Mountbatten for the Partition of British India was approaching. As the clock ticked down, Tony was taking local leave and like many of his fellow officers he chose the picturesque capital of Kashmir, Srinagar, enjoying the luxury of a houseboat on Dal Lake. On one excursion, he met friends at Gulmarg, west of Srinagar in the Pir Panjal hills, as it happened on the very day of Partition, 15th August 1947. Tony recalled of this meeting:[2] *"As we met, we realised that we were in the midst of great events. Terrible things were happening. Hari Singh, the Maharaja of Jammu and Kashmir, had signed an Accession document with India.[3] We heard through the servants that the Muslim Poonch tribe to our south had risen against their ruler spontaneously. We needed to get back to Fort Sandeman. Travelling down to Quetta was out of the question. Train loads of dead Muslims were arriving in Lahore and in turn train loads of dead Hindus were heading in the other direction. It was therefore necessary to get back to Fort Sandeman by a roundabout way through tribal territories to the west."*

Back in Fort Sandeman, Tony together with his brother officers adapted to life after Partition. Initially, British generals were chosen to command the newly established Indian and Pakistani armies. General

---

[2] This and subsequent recollections are taken from an interview with Tony conducted by Conrad Wood for the Imperial War Museum in 1986, IWM reference 080600000404.

[3] Hari Singh, the Maharaja of Jammu and Kashmir, actually signed the Accession document with India later, on 26 October 1947.

Douglas Gracey was C-in-C of the Pakistan Army whilst General Lockhart was C-in-C of the Indian Army, with Field Marshal Auchinleck as Supreme Commander of both Armies. However, the new Indian government was anxious to remove all traces of British rule and this included replacing most of the serving British officers with Indian officers. In contrast, the new Dominion of Pakistan, in which Tony now found himself, kept many of the British officers.

This was accomplished in two steps. Each British officer first had to join the British Army, in the process choosing a British Army regiment. Tony chose the Gloucestershire Regiment because, he claimed, it represented the county with the best hunting potential. Then followed a secondment to the officer's respective Pakistani unit. As for the native soldiers in the old British Indian regiments, they were being split up and reassigned. The Rajputana Rifles were recalled to Delhi and became part of the Indian Army, except D Company which, being composed of Muslims, was absorbed into the newly formed Pakistan Army.

One of Tony's responsibilities at Fort Sandeman was the procurement of remounts, the task of maintaining the Scouts with a supply of fresh horses. This required him to attend the two annual horse fairs near the towns of Peshawar and Rawalpindi. It was whilst visiting one of these fairs, or perhaps at the Mona Remount Depot itself, that he made the acquaintance of Sir Ambrose Dundas Flux Dundas. Dundas had been Defence Secretary to the Viceroy in Delhi but chose to serve the new Dominion of Pakistan after Partition. In 1948 he was appointed Governor of the North-West Frontier Province, the last British officer to hold that post. Sir Ambrose remembered meeting the young officer from Fort Sandeman and asked Tony to be his ADC. Tony left Fort Sandeman and would serve under Sir Ambrose until the latter's position was taken by a Pakistan national a year later.

As ADC to the Governor of the North-West Frontier Province, Tony found himself witnessing much political intrigue. Notionally he was now in the Tochi Scouts which were based at Peshawar, the town in which the Governor was based, and he was working with the Governor on a daily basis and meeting leading politicians and local rulers. The most distinguished of course was Muhammad Ali Jinnah, the first leader of independent Pakistan, a man, Tony remarked, who commanded your instant respect even if he was difficult to talk to. Another was Lt Col Syed Shahid Hamid, who had been Private Secretary to the C-in-C of the Indian Army, Field Marshal Sir Claude Auchinleck. Coincidentally, on days off in Delhi when he was still with the Rajputana Rifles, Tony had been introduced to Auchinleck and indeed also to Wavell, then the Viceroy, when both Field Marshals sought a few hours of respite in a friendly Officers' Mess from the burgeoning political quagmire engulfing the Indian subcontinent. Shahid Hamid and his family remained forever close to Tony.[4]

On two occasions as ADC, Tony had to intervene in the internal politics of the small state of Chitral in the mountainous north-west area of the North-West Frontier Province. On the death of the old Mehtar, or ruler, of Chitral, the mantle passed to his younger son who started creating trouble through a matrimonial dispute with the ruling family of the Dir clan to the south. Tony was ordered to remove the gentleman, which he effected by shepherding him to a waiting plane, placing him in the seat behind the pilot, and having him flown south to Rawalpindi. On another occasion he was ordered to arrest and remove an unpopular Assistant Political Officer, whom he promptly dispatched in a similar manner.

---

[4] Syed Shahid Hamid eventually became a Major General in the Pakistan Army and in retirement a historian of note. He was a grandfather of the British journalist Mishal Husein.

Captain HRA Streather, Chitral Scouts, with Captain A S Mathieson and Major W A Brown, ex-Commandant of the Gilgit Scouts, ca. 1949. In 1947 during the chaos following Partition, Willie Brown singlehandedly handed the entire Gilgit Agency to Pakistan.

Courtesy of Margaret Rosemary Brown
and Kate Brown.

When it was time to move back to the Frontier Scouts, which were now under Pakistani command, Tony was drawn by the mountains and requested a posting to the Chitral Scouts. During his Kashmir leave, Tony and a fellow officer had collected together a small trekking team — a sirdar, pack ponies and cook — and set off north to see something of the country. Tony recalled: "*A few days' hard walking and we were at the top of the Tragbal Pass just as the sun came up. We were rewarded by the most incredible sight. Just in front of us, looking as though we could almost touch it, was the whole of the south-east face of Nanga Parbat. This sight made an enormous impact on me and, without my realising it at the time, could well have been the start of my mountaineering career.*"

The state of Chitral had been established at the time of the Great Game and was defined by the Durand Line Agreement. To the east of Chitral lay the much larger state of Gilgit which Tony had got to know through his friendship with Willie Brown, the Commandant of the Gilgit Scouts, whom he had first met on leave in Srinagar. Tony's position was as second-in-command of the Chitral Scouts who were tasked with policing the dangerous tribal territories along the Afghan frontier. He found himself travelling in high, rugged and often snow-covered mountain country, and being fluent in Pushtu he interacted easily with its inhabitants. He was soon to add a smattering of the local Chitrali dialect, Khowar. Already captivated by the mountains, Tony was in his element. An additional attraction of Chitral was polo. The constant contact with horses in Fort Sandeman had given Tony an introduction to the original 'Sport of Kings'. It was played on dirt grounds, with players mounted on hardy mountain ponies. In Chitral, it was a matter of honour for each village to field a polo team. Tony's love of the sport lasted throughout his army career.

And for a third time, Tony had to remove an undesirable from Chitral. Now it was the distinguished Editor of the Calcutta newspaper *The Statesman*, Ian Stephens, who was suspected, mistakenly, of making an unauthorized visit. As Stephens narrates in his autobiographical narrative *Horned Moon*:[5] "... *the then Mehtar of Chitral, unmistakably though obliquely, had shown I was unwelcome. Two successive emissaries from him had conveyed messages: first his private secretary, then — with embarrassment — the young British Commandant of the Chitral Scouts. Fighting, they politely explained on his behalf, was at that time going on between India and Pakistan in nearby Kashmir; Chitral had acceded to Pakistan; the newspaper which I represented was published in India ...*" In short, Stephens was suspected of spying. In fact, he was already an ardent supporter of Pakistan and as the years passed became a good friend of Tony's.

Tony remained with the Chitral Scouts until the end of 1950 when his time in Pakistan came to an end, and he, with the half-dozen British officers who had remained in the tribal territories, caught the troopship back to the UK to start another chapter in their military careers. He went for a final evening ride into the hills, accompanied by his spaniels, Oggie and Danny. On the back of Tony's saddle rode Beezu, an adopted monkey, who perhaps sensing that this was the end of his master's time, jumped off his mount with a great chattering and scampered off to rejoin a troop of monkeys in the trees.

---

[5] Ian Stephens, 1953, *Horned Moon*, Chatto and Windus, London.

The Norwegian Expedition to Tirich Mir — 1950

Following the discovery of Everest, 29,028 feet, by the Survey of India, the British were regarded as having the first call on that mightiest of peaks. With attempts led by the Duke of the Abruzzi to K2 in 1909 and the Duke of Spoleto in 1927, the Italians claimed rights to K2, 28,250 feet high in the Karakoram, and meanwhile Germany through repeated attempts claimed Nanga Parbat, 26,659 feet.[6]

A little to the west of Nanga Parbat lies Tirich Mir, a somewhat lesser mountain but still a formidable 25,288-foot peak with no obvious claim from the international climbing fraternity. Tirich Mir is the highest peak of the Hindu Kush range, and its summit dominates the District of Chitral. But it was only after 1927 that the Survey of India undertook a detailed survey of Chitral and determined the height of the peak. About that time Colonel Lawder, then Commandant of the Chitral Scouts, carried out a reconnaissance on the mountain and formed the opinion that while approaching the summit from the north was altogether impracticable there was a feasible line on the mountain's south flanks, on which the successful attempt was subsequently made.

However, there were other less tractable impediments at play. There was a widespread belief among Chitrali locals that Tirich Mir harboured powerful spirits and that any attempt to climb the mountain would result in evil spells being cast on anyone trespassing on the mountain's slopes. In particular, it was believed that a mythical frog of enormous size called *Bogazu* would drag climbers into deep crevasses in which it was said to reside. Approaching Tirich Mir therefore

---

[6] Heights in feet are quoted from the Himalayan index (http://www.alpine-club.org.uk/hi/) for the wider Himalayan ranges and from Wikipedia for elsewhere. They may therefore differ from heights originally quoted in various sources.

required overcoming these superstitions and certainly before local porters could be engaged to accompany any serious expedition attempting the mountain.

Tony wearing the colours of Norway on his rucksack on the lower slopes of Tirich Mir.

Courtesy of the Streather family.

Such was the amateur approach of this team that they spent a night and a day in the customs sheds of Bombay with their luggage as they had no money for a night in a hotel! The Indian porters were amazed at these *pukka sahibs*, who insisted on carrying their own baggage. After many adventures, during which they had to exit India and enter Pakistan, they eventually reached Nathia Gali, a summer resort in the foothills northeast of Rawalpindi. In Nathia Gali and later in Chitral they met many locals and British officials who provided assistance, but one in particular stood out, a certain Captain Streather. Professor Arne Næss wrote of meeting him:[7] "*A young Captain Streather was among many in Nathia Gali, who was really distressed at not being able to join us on our Tirich Mir trip. He had been invaluable in digging out maps for us. He was supposed to be a bit absent-minded, but in fact it was simply that during our touching farewell when the bus was about to roll down to Nathia Gali, the entire money supply of the expedition had vanished. It turned out that I had left it in Streather's map room, and he had not discovered this immediately.*"

Tony subsequently wrote: "*When I was serving in Chitral and a Norwegian party came out to attempt Tirich Mir, I remembered my first sight of Nanga Parbat and had no hesitation in trying to work my way onto the team in one capacity or another. I could speak the local language and knew the country well, so I offered to be their Transport Officer.*"

After the exploratory team returned to Norway, the Norwegian Alpine Club had to decide whether to mount a full expedition the following year. Opinions were mixed, and other climbing groups in Europe were also interested. In January 1950, Næss was informed that an Anglo-Swiss party was contemplating going to Tirich Mir in 1950,

---

[7] Arne Næss and others, 1952, *The Norwegian Himalaya Expedition - Tirich Mir*, Hodder and Stoughton, London.

but that the Norwegians had first refusal provided they were ready to leave by May.

Tony with three Norwegians members. Arne Næss, the expedition leader, and colleagues were surprised to see Tony sometimes carrying his full load of tent and mattress up the mountain.

Courtesy of the Streather family.

The Club settled on a team consisting of five Norwegian Alpine Club members, a doctor and two scientists chosen by the Norwegian Geographical Society. And it was agreed to invite two members from Pakistan, Professor Abdul Hamid Beg, who was the President of the Lahore Climbing Club, and Captain Streather. The expedition's baggage weighed three tons and left Oslo on the last day of March 1950. The team left by air two months later. Their arrival in Karachi, then still the capital of the new state of Pakistan, was somewhat better organised than that of the reconnaissance team the previous year.

The Norwegians had brought currency notes, but Tony explained that the porters would insist on being paid in coin due their mistrust of paper money. All the notes had to be exchanged for a mountain of coins and counted out in Tony's office. Professor Næss's account of the expedition shows a photograph of Tony (see page 23). It is the only photo of him in Scouts uniform, which appears to consist simply of a pair of native trousers and shirt-like top and a Chitrali hat with the ibex horns badge of the Chitral Scouts.

Tony, who had no technical mountaineering experience, quickly made himself indispensable as a Mr Fixit, able to deal with the inevitable bureaucracy and managing the selection of porters for both the walk-in and mountain load carrying. As an aside, because of Partition, Sherpas were not available to assist the Norwegians, so Hunza porters, whose reputation had already been established in the Karakoram, together with local Chitral porters, provided the expedition's porterage. Tony's local knowledge and language skills ensured that the team reached Base Camp at 10,500 feet on the Barum Glacier without major incident through an area hitherto untouched by mountaineering expeditions.

Professor Beg wrote: "*The Norwegians were surprised that on the approach march Tony wore his Chitral Scouts regulation chaplis — open-toed, leather sandals — and though he was not expected to go high, were delighted when he powered up the mountain with them in his battledress, pyjamas and hob-nailed army boots ... with a resting heartbeat in the mid-40s, he was obviously a powerful performer at altitude.*"

Base camp for the ascent was established in a green and fertile valley set in the otherwise arid foothills. It was named the *Idyell*, and Tony brought there his dog and a squad of soldiers who set up a tent, radio mast, and a small generator to ensure connection with Charlie Five, the expedition's contact radio station. However, he also brought an item which caused the Norwegians some misgivings. Professor Næss: "*We had also to stomach a gramophone. It had been handed down through the years among the English soldiers in Chitral and so had the needles. At the end of our stay at Idyllen, it was impossible to distinguish between 'Ave Maria', and Bing Crosby's 'Ain't got a dime to my name'*".

Tony was slowly assimilated into the Norwegian team. He said of his joining the Norwegians:[8]

"*I literally had never tied on a rope before, but of course I had spent months crossing passes, living in the mountains at reasonable altitudes — I was very fit indeed. I had no major ambitions. Initially, I was there to organise the porters. I think the Norwegians had this idea of the British Colonial exploiting the porters and expecting me to go round beating the locals.*" On the mountain and speaking Khowar, Streather managed to persuade the porters ever higher, but only by accompanying them himself. Rather to his surprise, "*It really was by accident that I ended up on top.*"

A first attempt on the summit took place on 3rd July 1950, but it took its toll on the Norwegian climbers. They were experienced in their own mountains and the Alps but not the high mountains of the Hindu Kush. For the second attempt, non-Norwegian Tony was asked to join the team. He recalls the moment: "*One thing led to another. One of the climbers was taken ill with what was thought at the time to be pneumonia but which today would have been recognised as pulmonary oedema. This bad luck for him was good luck for me and gave me the chance to join the summit team.*"

In the end six were included in this final assault. One of the team,

---

[8] Jim Curran, 2013, *Army Dreamer ... a Portrait of Tony Streather*, http://footlesscrow.blogspot.com/2013/11/army-dreamer-portrait-of-tony-streather.html

who had gone on ahead, was actually the first to reach the summit a day before the others. The following day, Næss and the others reached the summit at sunset. As Næss describes it: "*We could easily have run the last few steps for sheer joy. We had a kind of cairn ceremony in good Norwegian style. But we had still to hoist the four flags of Norway, the United Nations, Pakistan and a colossal Union Jack which Streather had dragged with him. This was the only size procurable in Chitral!*" There is a photograph in the Alpine Journal of Tony trying his best to control this huge flag in the winds on the summit. Tony later commented: "*And so my first peak became Tirich Mir. I had no idea at the time that I had become the first Englishman to reach the summit of a 25,000-foot peak.*"[9]

Intermediate camp on Tirich Mir.
Courtesy of the Streather family.

---

[9] Tony inadvertently failed to remember that in 1936 Noel Odell and Bill Tilman had climbed Nanda Devi, being at 25,643 feet just 354 feet higher than Tirich Mir.

Unfurling flags on the summit of Tirich Mir. As Arne Næss handled the Norwegian, Pakistan and UN flags, Tony struggled with a huge Union Jack, the only size locally available in Chitral.

Alpine Club Photo Library, London.

On the return journey to Karachi, Tony used his influence to obtain rooms for the team in the prestigious Peshawar Club — a British officer still had his uses to pull the necessary strings. It was the last service he rendered to them and was no doubt a small factor in the Honorary Membership of the Norwegian Alpine Club with which he was later rewarded. Invited to dinners given by the Club annually, he greatly enjoyed meeting up again with his Norwegian comrades. Tony kept in touch with Professor Arne Næss until the latter's death in January 2009 and subsequently with his wife, Kit-Fai Næss. The team members had planned a trip to Tirich Mir in 2000, but at the age of 88 Arne was not in the best of health, so the trip had to be cancelled. By then, Arne was known internationally as a leading environmentalist.

For Tony, the Tirich Mir expedition held one more bonus. When he returned to the United Kingdom, he was invited to join the prestigious Alpine Club — intriguing for him, as he imagined that it was merely some sort of superannuated club for gentlemen. At that time, the Alpine Club was based in Mayfair, and as one member remarked, if one pressed the wrong doorbell one was likely to find oneself in the Egyptian Embassy. The criterion for membership was exacting — thirty good summits in the Alps or Greater Ranges and at least three years' mountaineering experience. On these criteria, Tony certainly did not qualify. However, for someone who had almost set a height record for an Englishman, there was definitely room for manoeuvre.

Tony was proposed by Colonel Tobin, late Indian Army himself and one of the prime movers of the Himalayan Club when it was established in 1928. "I'll get Longstaff to second you," he explained.[10] Tony continues:[11] *"I had no idea of the honour that was being extended to me nor what a privilege it was that Dr Tom Longstaff, who was the retiring President, should himself be interested in me. I learned later of his long connection with the parts of the world where I had been serving and of his distinguished mountaineering career. He was extremely kind to me and advised me on how to complete my application form. One peak was hardly enough, even though it was a pretty high one. What else had I done so that we could make the form look a little better? We settled, in the end, on several years of scrambling in Baluchistan, Waziristan, Gilgit, Chitral and Kashmir, all areas he knew well. That seemed to be enough for the Committee and I was elected."*

---

[10] Tom Longstaff was President of the Alpine Club from 1947 to 1949.
[11] Tony Streather, *President's Valedictory Address*, read before the Alpine Club on 4 December 1992: Alpine Club Journal, vol. 98: 1-6, 1993.

K2, the Savage Mountain — 1953

Now back in the UK, Tony was posted to the Warminster School of Infantry as an Army instructor. In late 1952 he received an interesting letter. In his own words: *"The same Colonel Tobin, who had proposed me for membership of the Alpine Club, now wrote again saying that I should think about applying to join the expedition that was being planned to attempt Everest in 1953. I had, after all, proved that I could go high even if I was not much of a climber. It was arranged that I should meet Eric Shipton, who at that time was going to lead [the expedition]. I had in fact met him briefly before, when he passed through Peshawar on his way home from his appointment as our Consul-General in Kashgar. He now kindly invited me to lunch at his home in Sussex. When I arrived he was gardening. He was combining this with training for the mountains. He had a large old rucksack which he filled with earth at the bottom of the garden and then carried up the hill to the top of the garden where he was preparing a new flower bed. It would be like him to scorn the use of a simple wheelbarrow. The upshot of this meeting was that I was asked to join four other potential members of the expedition, all of whom were experienced alpinists, for a trip to the Alps.*

"I had only been there once before on a brief skiing holiday. I thoroughly enjoyed myself but clearly did not impress the others. There may have been some slight resentment that the altitude seemed to have no effect on me whatsoever, but what really let me down was my inept fumbling when the time came to put on crampons. I had hardly used the things on Tirich Mir, and this now became all too obvious. The other four were all to become members or reserves, but clearly my lack of Alpine experience had disqualified me. I received a brief note from the Everest Office telling me so, but there was little time for disappointment. Almost

by the same post came a letter from Dr Houston in America inviting me to join his team to K2 as Transport Officer and then to climb with them as high as I wished or was able."

K2 expedition members: standing (l-r) Tony Streather, Charlie Houston, Bob Craig, George Bell, Bill White (with NBC), Pete Schoening, Bob Bates; seated (l-r) Dee Molenaar, Art Gilkey, Lt Zaffir (local military interpreter), Col Ata Ullah.

Courtesy of the Streather family.

Tony's success with the Norwegians had brought him to the attention of the American Dr Charles Houston who was planning his second attempt on K2, the second highest mountain after Everest. By now, Tony had the reputation of someone who could command the respect of Pakistani local porters as well as having a track record of climbing high. Ironically, as even the most amateur followers of climbing would have been aware, K2 was technically far more demanding than Everest. Tony's ineptitude with crampons clearly didn't bother Houston.

K2 was originally known as Mt. Godwin-Austen after Major-General Henry Godwin-Austen, an English surveyor of the mid-19th century. The first attempt on the summit was made by a party in July 1902 consisting of three Englishmen, two Australians and a Swiss doctor. The Duke of the Abruzzi followed in 1909 with an ambitious expedition that also failed to climb K2 but claimed a height record for that time on a nearby peak. The first American expedition was led by the young Dr Charles Houston in 1938, followed shortly afterwards by a second American expedition led by Fritz Weissner in 1939 that reached within 1,000 feet of the summit but ended in tragedy.

The Second World War and then Partition initially prevented any further attempts. But nothing would dissuade Dr Houston, who used his longstanding friendship with the then US ambassador to Pakistan to seek a return to K2. Eventually permission was given for Dr Houston to lead a party in 1953. With two exceptions, this was to be an all-American team of good all-rounders, experienced on both snow and ice. The only non-Americans were liaison officer Colonel Ata Ullah of the Pakistan Army and Tony Streather.

Tony was described by expedition member Bob Craig in the book *K2 - The Savage Mountain,* which Houston and he co-wrote, in the following terms:[12] "*Tony was a twenty-seven-year old officer in the First Battalion of the Gloucestershire Regiment, who had reached the summit of Tirich Mir several hundred miles west of K2 with a Norwegian expedition in 1950. Houston had corresponded with him, their letters had led to friendship, and he had been accepted unseen. Within a few*

---

[12] Charles S Houston, M.D. and Robert H. Bates, 1954, *K2 – the Savage Mountain*, McGraw-Hill, New York.

days of our meeting in Pakistan, Streather was one of the most popular members. His disposition never changed, he told fabulous tales of the North-West Frontier country. Best of all, he was not only an excellent transport officer, which was his primary responsibility, but he soon became one of the party's strongest packers and climbers."

K2: Tony, without shirt, supervising a river crossing at Gue on the approach march.

Courtesy of the Streather family.

43

Following Partition, Sherpa porters were not available, so reliance would be placed on Hunza porters who did not have the same experience at high altitude. There was no funding for the expedition by either the US Government or the American climbing fraternity. With support of friends, the team had to raise $25,000, and at least a quarter was raised from expedition members themselves. What contribution Tony was able to make is unknown. Certainly not helping Tony's financial situation was the Army's rule that during leave, even if it could be argued to provide valuable mountain training, a soldier was obliged to forfeit pay and pension contributions.

Following his return to the UK, Tony gave an account of this third American expedition to K2 in an address to the Alpine Club on 2nd February 1954, later published in both the *Alpine Journal* and the *Himalayan Journal*. Since this expedition has become so renowned, it is perhaps best to hear Tony's version:[13] *"Towards the end of 1952, I was invited by Dr. Charles Houston to join an expedition he was organising to make an attempt on K2, the second highest mountain in the world. I had served for some time in the North of Pakistan and had a fair knowledge of the people there and of their languages. My job was to be that of Transport Officer. I was to make the arrangements to get the expedition to its Base Camp and was then to become a member of the climbing party.*

"Naturally I accepted this invitation with the greatest of pleasure and welcomed the opportunity of returning north to the passes of Pakistan. The problem of obtaining the necessary leave from the Army was not so easy. However, this difficulty was overcome, and I was granted special

---

[13] H R A Streather, 1954, *Third American Karakoram Expedition – K2*, The Himalayan Journal, vol. XVIII: 67-80; also Alpine Journal, vol. LIX, no. 289: 391-401.

long leave to join the expedition.

"K2, sometimes called Mount Godwin-Austen, rises to 28,250 feet in the remote country to the north of Baltistan on the unmarked borders of the Chinese province of Sinkiang. It narrowly upholds its claim to be the second highest mountain in the world, for Kangchenjunga is barely a hundred feet lower.

"K2 was first noted for its great height by Captain Montgomerie in 1856, while he was working with the Survey of India. Since then it has been seen by many great travellers but few attempts have been made to climb it. The first of these was in 1902 when Eckenstein reached a height of 21,000 feet on the north-east spur. The famous Italian explorer, Prince Luigi Amedeo of Savoy, Duke of the Abruzzi, led a large expedition to the Karakoram in 1909 and, besides much other fine work, made an attempt on K2. He decided to try by the south-east ridge and three of his guides, after a very difficult climb, reached a height of rather more than 20,000 feet, 'towards a reddish rock,' before deciding that it was useless to proceed further. Later they reached a height of 21,870 feet. on the western spur, above the saddle which later became known as the Savoia Pass. The Duke eventually decided that further efforts to climb K2 would be hopeless. After that, K2 was seen by Dr. Longstaff, the Bullock-Workmans, the Duke of Spoleto, Dyhrenfurth, H. de Ségogne and others, but no further attempts to climb it were made until twenty-nine years later, when in 1938 Dr. Houston led an American expedition in a determined effort to find a route to the summit.

"Enough cannot be said of the good work and perseverance of this expedition. After many weeks of reconnaissance and after making bids on several of the ridges, they made a last determined effort up the south-east ridge, named then the Abruzzi Ridge, after the Duke who had tried it twenty-nine years before. They reached the 'reddish rock' referred to by

the Duke and this proved to be the key to the whole problem. A small and extremely steep chimney led to the top of this red rock. Bill House made a very fine lead and after a hard climb reached the top of the chimney. From then on they had worked slowly forward until Houston and Petzoldt had eventually reached a height of about 26,000 feet before having to turn back. They had spent many weeks on the mountain and believed they had found a possible route to the summit.

"*The following year a further American expedition led by Wiessner tried the same route. Wiessner himself reached a height of a little over 26,000 feet but the expedition ended in tragedy and one American and three Sherpas lost their lives. Little has been written of the gallant efforts of Pasang Kikuli, who with two other Sherpas attempted to rescue the abandoned American at Camp VII. None of them were seen again.*

"*Towards the end of May 1953, we assembled in Rawalpindi and most of us met each other for the first time. I had come out by sea and had spent a few days travelling round Pakistan, seeing old friends; the others had flown out from the States. We all stayed there with Colonel Ata Ullah, who proved to be such a great comfort to us later by his consistent support and encouragement from Base Camp.*

"*Our party was a strong one. Charles Houston, the leader, was already well known for his wonderful achievements in 1938. He had also climbed in 1936 on Nanda Devi and might have been one of the summit pair had he not eaten a bad tin of food at the high camp. Bob Bates was also with him in 1938 and this year again did a fine job with our commissariat. He had climbed extensively during the last twenty-two years in Alaska and the Yukon. George Bell, a theoretical physicist and a tough six-footer, had distinguished himself on Yerupaja (21,679 feet) and Salcantay (20,574 feet), two peaks in Peru, which had not been previously climbed. Then there was Art Gilkey, a geologist from Iowa, a man with great drive and determination. Dee Molenaar and Bob Craig, both from Seattle, were ski and climbing instructors at the Army Mountain School. Craig had climbed Mount McKinley. Pete Schoening, also from Seattle, was a great expert in the art of belaying and this proved very fortunate for us all later. With these seven American members in the party were Colonel Ata Ullah and myself. The Colonel was nearly fifty but this did not prevent him climbing with us to our Camp III, and visiting Windy Gap at a little over 20,000 feet, at the head of the K2 Glacier. Only three of us had climbed in the Himalayas. Houston and Bates on K2 in 1938 and Houston, before that, on Nanda Devi in 1936. I had climbed Tirich Mir, with the Norwegians in 1950.*

"This was the party which assembled in Rawalpindi and prepared to set off from there on the long journey to Skardu and then the march to Base Camp.

"We were able to fly the first stage of our journey and land on the rather frightening airfield at Skardu. This was a most impressive flight. We passed close under the walls of Nanga Parbat and one of us even claimed that he was able to see the tracks of the German expedition which was later successful in climbing that mountain. On up the narrow gorge we passed Rakaposhi and Haramosh, with a brief glimpse of K2 away to the north and then we landed at last at Skardu to breathe that cool sweet air which seems only to exist in the great mountain ranges. It was hard to believe that we had reached Skardu in but a few hours when, in the days before the Partition in India, this same journey had entailed a long trek of many days from Srinagar over the Zoji La or across the Deosai Plains.

"We were given a hearty reception in Skardu and the main street of the bazaar was brightly decorated and crowded as we passed through. The banners displayed by the school children and the conversation of leading citizens made us fully aware of the strong feeling in this area over

the bitter Kashmir problem. Skardu had been the scene of much fighting in 1947 and had changed hands several times.

"We were most hospitably entertained by the Political Agent and the Officers of the Northern Scouts, who did everything possible to help us prepare for the next stage of our journey. Coolies were employed, some of our loads were repacked, and food was purchased for the porters who would be remaining with us to work on the mountain. The Mir of Hunza had kindly selected a few good men and he had sent these down to join us at Skardu. One of them had climbed with me on Tirich Mir in 1950. This was the first time that Hunza porters had been employed to a large extent on a major expedition and they were to prove themselves in every way worthy.

"On June 5 all was ready, and having crossed the Indus in 'Alexander's Barge', we set out on our two-week trek to Base Camp. For the first few stages we marched up the fertile Shighar valley and then, a little above the village of Bahar, we were forced to cross to the north bank of the Braldu River.

"The coolies, recruited from the villages around Skardu and the lower Shighar villages, said that the track on the south bank was no longer safe for laden men. Nothing would persuade them to change their minds and we were forced to accept a delay of nearly two days while we laboriously ferried all our kit across the river on a very inadequate goatskin raft.

"In Skardu I had drawn up a very careful contract for the supply and payment of coolies with a man recommended to me by the Political Agent. It was during the delay in crossing the river that I realised what a rogue this contractor was. He was giving the coolies but a fraction of their pay and pocketing the rest himself. Each day coolies would become more and more difficult to find and as we arrived in a village·all the fit men *would disappear, for fear of being pressed into labour with us. As soon as I realised what was going on, I sacked the contractor and from that day on all went well. In fact, at most of the villages where we stopped for the night, men would crowd round us and fight for the loads when the time came to set out on the next stage of our journey the following morning.*

"After crossing two of the infamous rope bridges, both in very bad repair, we eventually reached Askole, the last village in the Braldu valley. We were given a great reception here, where the older men wanted to know if we knew the 'Duke Sahib' and the slightly less old if we knew 'Shipton Sahib'!

"We had fun here making tape recordings of the villagers singing and then playing their own songs back to them over our radio. The following morning the whole village wanted to accompany us, but whether this was because of the novel entertainment we provided or because of the good money they hoped we would pay, we couldn't say.

"As we moved on up the Baltoro glacier the novelty was wearing a little thin and twice impressive 'sit down' strikes were staged. The cry would be 'the Duke Sahib stopped here so we are going to,' even if we had only been marching a few hours. Spoleto I suppose — hardly Abruzzi! However, the strike leaders were prepared to listen to sense and we moved on without any increase in the settled pay …

"We reached our Base Camp on June 19, at about 16,500 feet, at the foot of the south ridge of K2. From here we sent back our coolies, only the six Hunza porters and ourselves remained. Fifty of our most loyal coolies were given instructions to come back and collect us on August 10. All these men had come from the village of Satpora near Skardu. This village had already made a name for itself by providing willing and loyal coolies for previous expeditions and they certainly earned our gratitude and respect that summer.

49

"Our first morning in Base Camp dawned bright and clear and as we unpacked and sorted our loads we had a wonderful view of the icy precipices and rocky ridges of K2 hanging over us to the north. We could follow the line of the Abruzzi Ridge, running steeply, horribly steeply, up to the snow shoulder at about 26,000 feet. This shoulder seemed to be the first and only 'let up' on the steep ridge before it verged into the summit cone.

"We started at once, working a tortuous route up the glacier, through the ice fall, to our Camp I at the very foot of the Abruzzi Ridge. After further hard days of relaying loads, the first two camps were eventually established on the ridge – Camp II at 19,300 feet and Camp III at 20,500 feet.

"Camp II was our last site of any size and was the last place where there was room for the Hunzas to live as well as the climbers. They carried loads with us to Camp III but from then on, all the carrying had to be done by ourselves … The risk of stone falls on the steep ridge was too great to allow for one 'ferry service' to work above the other, so we all had to climb together or wait in the sheltered camp sites until the ridge was clear. For these reasons we were convinced that we would not be justified in taking the Hunzas above Camp III.

"Camp III consisted of two tents, perched perilously on ledges we had cut from the ridge. It was here that we experienced our first storm which was but a foretaste of what was to come. We continued relaying our loads forward and on July 16 established Camp IV at the foot of House's Chimney, the 'reddish rock' which the Duke of the Abruzzi's guides had hoped to reach many years before. Camp V at 22,500 feet was only some 500 feet above Camp IV, but at that altitude it was a hard task to struggle up the chimney. We pulled our loads up on a pulley frame, which we had brought and erected for this purpose.

K2: Tony clearing the tent at Camp III after a storm.

Courtesy of the Streather family.

"Once above the chimney we felt that we really were getting somewhere at last. The climb to Camp VI, 23,400 feet, was again a short one and this camp was fully established, with all of us there, by the end of July."

The book *K2—the Savage Mountain* includes a sketch which shows the locations of the eight camps leading up the Abruzzi Ridge. The ascent of the ridge and the pitching of each of the planned camps was a slow task. There was little margin for error especially in the quantities of supplies which had been calculated to the nearest ounce. Some logistical problems were eased by the discovery of equipment abandoned by the 1939 expedition. Even sleeping bags, which when dried out after fourteen years' exposure, proved to be a blessing later in the expedition.

K2: Tony climbing on mixed rocks and snow between Camps VI and VII.
Courtesy of the Streather family.

As Tony describes: "*We had found other traces of the previous expedition during the climb but it was at Camp VI that we first found any evidence on the last hours of Pasang Kikuli and the Sherpas who climbed alone from Base Camp, in 1939, in an attempt to rescue Wolfe from Camp VII. We found the remains of two tents and inside them, neatly rolled ready for a move, were the sleeping bags and a few personal belongings of those gallant heroes. It was clear that they had prepared everything for their descent before going to VII, for a second time, to try to bring Wolfe down. "During the days that we had been establishing Camp VI, the weather had been deteriorating but we continued to climb and build our 'pyramid' during the bright spells. All previous records indicated that the monsoon had little effect in the Karakoram, and we did not believe that this was more than a local spell of bad weather. We did not expect more than a few stormy days before the promised clear, bright days would come.*

"The slab rock, covered with a thin layer of snow and ice, made the climb above Camp VI treacherous, but we carried loads to the point where Camp VII had been established in 1938 and where we hoped to make our own camp. However, the formation of the seracs at the foot of the snow shoulder had changed so much that no level site could be found for a camp. A narrow ledge was cut out in the snow slope, just wide enough for our smallest tent and two men stayed up here to seek further for a suitable camp site. The rest of us dumped our loads and climbed down again to VI. Camp VII thus became merely a cache.

"Gilkey and Schoening, who remained at VII, searched for the whole of the following day and eventually informed us at Camp VI, by walkie-talkie radio, that they had found a perfect camp site but that it was several hundred feet above the old Camp VII site. We later estimated the height of this camp, Camp VIII, to be 25,500 feet. This meant that we had a long climb, with loads, from Camp VI at 23,400 feet to Camp VIII at 25,500 feet.

"On August 1, we had sufficient loads at Camp VIII to justify four of the party moving up. Two were already there. The weather was still not good but surely the break would come soon! Bates and I remained that day in support at VI, for the climb to VIII would be a long one and if the weather remained bad, they might be forced, by the cold, to fall back on us. Late in the afternoon we heard that all had reached VIII safely and had established a strong camp there.

"The following day dawned clear and sunny and we hoped that this would be the chance we had been waiting for. Bates and I struck Camp VI and, leaving tents and food for our return safely stored on one of the ledges, set out on the long climb to Camp VIII. The same day those already at VIII came down to the cache at VII to collect further supplies. Soon after we had started the weather once again deteriorated and before long we were climbing in appalling conditions. At about midday, we heard the others shouting to us from the cache, when we were tackling the treacherous ice-covered slabs of 'the black pyramid' as we called this pitch. From the glacier below it had looked most formidable and exposed. We reached the cache after the others had returned to Camp VIII; fortunately they had carefully marked the route up the snow with willow wands. The weather was now atrocious, but we had come too far to think of turning back. Night was falling fast when we eventually sighted Camp VIII through the driving snow. With relief we crowded into one of the mountain tents and welcomed the hot drink which was ready for us. We had been climbing for over 10 hours.

"We were all of us at Camp VIII now, and with food and fuel to last us for at least ten days. We had behind us a well-stocked line of camps, and down at Base, in touch with us by wireless, were the Colonel Ata Ullah and our six Hunza porters. In spite of the efforts of the last few days we were all in extremely good condition and had acclimatised well. Our *gear was in good shape and morale was high. Most of the difficult climbing was over and we were less than 3,000 feet from the summit. All we needed now was a break in the weather, just three days might be enough, so that we could put the last part of our plan into action. Our basic plan was simple. On the first clear day we would all carry loads to Camp IX, which we hoped to establish at about 27,000 feet. The strongest two climbers would go ahead with light loads and reconnoitre the route. These two would remain at Camp IX, with supplies for several days, and would make a bid for the summit on the next clear day. If they failed, a second pair would try, and there would still be time and food for a third or even a fourth pair if necessary. We had not planned to use oxygen, and we had none. The problem of carrying the extra loads up the steep ridge, without the help of a large number of porters, was too great and we did not consider oxygen essential to reach a summit at 28,250 feet.*

"We had already spent nearly a month above 20,500 feet, and far from deteriorating, we had been getting fitter from day to day. There were none of the usual signs of mountain sickness and we attributed this to the length of time we had been acclimatising with strenuous exercise, as we worked our way slowly forward from camp to camp. We had made six or more carries each, between most of the camps."

The tedium of establishing these high-altitude camps and the days spent sheltering from the storms were leavened by Tony's accounts of his soldiering, as described by Charles Houston: "*Discussion of the next move led us to reminiscence of things past, and soon Tony got off on tales of the frontier. For several hours he regaled us with accounts of intrigue and adventure with near escapes and capture during the war years and the hectic summer and fall of 1947 when India and Pakistan were divided. It was an exciting afternoon, for Streather had seen much and is a born raconteur.*"

But the weather was closing in. Tony's account continues: *"That night the storm continued with unrelenting ferocity and the wind seemed to have some personal malice against us, as though it was determined to blow us from the mountain. It continued through the following day. We were confined to our bags and unable even to talk to each other without shouting at the top of our voices. The stoves would not stay alight in the flapping tents, so we were not able to get more than a cup or two of liquid to drink; not nearly enough at that altitude.*

"On the morning of the August 4th, we heard a pathetic cry from outside, 'Help, our tent has gone.' Houston crawled in to join Bates and me while Bell joined two of the others. We were now eight of us in three small mountain tents.

"Every evening we spoke to the Colonel on our wireless and always he had received the same weather forecast from Radio Pakistan: 'Snow and storm.'

"So it continued until the morning of the 7th. I would be wrong to say that on that day we awoke to a bright morning, for there had been little sleep during the previous nights; but the clouds were clearing and the sun was shining although the wind was still blowing strongly. For the first time since our arrival at Camp VIII we were able to think of further movement. Bell and Molenaar had been slightly frost-bitten during the storm so they would go down. Bates and I would go down with them to Camp VII and bring up more food and fuel. The other four would kick steps up the snow slope and start working the route towards Camp IX. We would have to be more certain of the weather before we could think of establishing Camp IX, but we could start preparing the way.

"When we crawled from our tents, intent on continuing with this plan, Gilkey complained of pain in one of his legs. He tried to stand with his full weight on it but collapsed in a faint. Houston looked at it and

soon diagnosed thrombo-phlebitis. If Art was to have any chance of recovery we must get him down at once, there was nothing else for it. All our plans of going higher were abandoned and we set about preparing to carry Art down. We bundled him in sleeping bags, wrapped him in the torn tent and set off dragging him through the snow. We soon realised that we were in grave danger of starting an avalanche and we were forced to return and re-establish Camp VIII. Craig and Schoening set out to find an alternative route and reported a steep rock and ice ridge some hundred yards to the south of the snow slope. By this time the weather had again reverted to storm and further movement became impossible that day.

"The days passed but still the storm showed no signs of relenting. Each evening the forecast was bad. On the 10th of August we realised just how serious the situation had become. We were suffering particularly from dehydration, for we had not been able to melt much snow and we were suffering too from the effect of having spent ten very worrying days, cowering from the storm. I'm sure that our deterioration was due more to these factors than simply to altitude. Art was in a bad state. We must get him down as soon as possible. Both his legs were now affected and clots of blood had moved to his lungs.

"We wrapped him again in a sleeping bag and tent and set out, in the raging storm, to get him down by the new route. This was a desperate attempt, but we had no alternative. First, we dragged him a short way through the deep snow and then we lowered him down the steep ridge and ice slope below. After many hours of exhausting work, feeling extremely tired and cold, we had descended little more than 400 feet. Somehow we would all have to spend the night on the small ledge at Camp VII for there was no chance now of reaching Camp VI as we had hoped.

"We had just lowered Art over a steep rock cliff, when one of the climbers slipped. We were climbing, for the most part, in pairs and in some miraculous way our ropes crossed and became entangled. Five of us were pulled off the steep ice slope. Pete Schoening, who was at the time holding the rope on which we were lowering Art, had the only strong belay and somehow he held us all. [George] Bell had fallen more than 200 feet and the rest of us a little less. Again, by some miracle, none of us was badly hurt although Houston was unconscious for a time and Bell had badly frozen hands, through having lost his gloves in the fall. Those of us who were able, made our way to Camp VII and managed to erect a tent on the tiny platform there. We then helped the casualties to the shelter of this tent. During the rescue, Art had been left securely anchored on the snow slope by two ice axes."

"*While we were getting the others into shelter we were able to shout back and forth at Art, only about 200 feet away over a small rise; but we could not hear what he was saying, above the noise of the wind. He was very heavily drugged so that he would not know too much of the awful discomfort of the descent.*

"The rescue operation took about half an hour and then the three of us who could still move went back to try and do something for Art. We realised that we could not move him but we hoped to be able to cut a small ledge in the slope, feed him and help to make him comfortable for the night. When we got back he had gone. At first we could not believe our eyes but slowly we realised that a small avalanche had come down and taken him away. The surface of the slope was soft and broken. There was no trace of Art or of the axes which had anchored him.

"Once over the shock of having lost Art, we realised that his passing was a miraculous deliverance from a situation which might well have meant disaster for all of us. If we had continued the attempt to carry him

down over the increasingly difficult climbing below, it is most improbable that we could have avoided further and perhaps even more serious accidents.

"That night at Camp VII is the longest I can ever remember and certainly the worst I ever wish to spend. Four of us were squatting in one small mountain tent, on an even smaller ledge, and the other three of us in a tiny bivouac tent, with just a pole at one end. Charlie was delirious and would not keep still for a second except when he collapsed unconscious. He had cracked some ribs and his chest was paining him terribly and making it even harder for him to gasp the rarefied air. George Bell had frozen hands and feet and all of us had some degree of frostbite. Pete Schoening was exhausted from the effort of having held us all for some considerable time while we sorted ourselves out after the fall. I had some tea and sugar in the pocket of my parka and Bob Craig had a stove with him.

"We spent the night making tea and passing it round for all to sip. We were able to make pathetically little but it helped. We huddled in our tents, trying to warm our bare feet against the belly of the man next to us, and wondering what the morning would bring. The wind had ceased and the night was calm. This was almost the only kind thought that the mountain spared us until we were well below Base Camp many days later.

"Next morning we took stock and found seven very tired and battered climbers. We were determined to keep our heads and climb carefully down through the line of camps we had taken so long to build on the ridge. How Charlie and George climbed that day I shall never know. Charlie was still very dazed from his concussion and George's feet were in a bad state. But there were no slips and late that afternoon we reached Camp VI.*

"It was four days before we eventually reached Camp II. The descent had been slow and painful but now at least we were safe.

"I shall never forget our arrival at Camp II. The Hunzas were there to meet us and, as they heard us climbing down through the darkness of the evening, they came clambering up to meet us. We were literally carried the last few feet into camp and there a wonderful treat was awaiting us. The evening was calm and down here it was even warm enough to sit outside. We lay back on our sleeping bags among the rocks, our boots off, and our weary legs being massaged, while milk and rice and tea and then more tea were brought to us.

"The Hunzas did not hide their joy at seeing us safe again and many sincere tears were shed that evening. When we had eaten and drunk all our unaccustomed stomachs would take, we settled down to talk quietly among ourselves for the first time for many days. There was an almost tangible feeling of relief in the air. I told the Hunzas about Art, and they offered a most touching prayer in his memory and asked me to translate their feelings to the others. Although no sentimentalist, I found it hard to prevent my voice from breaking as I translated their thoughtful wishes of condolence to the Americans. No people from our so-called civilised countries could express themselves with such complete and unaffected sincerity as those six men from the remote Central Asian State of Hunza.

"Next morning, after breakfast in bed, there was mail to open and newspapers, a month or so old, to be read. Bob Bates and I set off ahead of the others, for our last climb down to Base Camp, to warn the Colonel of our arrival. We had lost one of our walkie-talkies in the fall and the battery of the other was flat, so we could not talk to him that day. The coolies from Satpora had already arrived and had been waiting for us at Base Camp for the past week.

"We received a wonderful reception from the Colonel, who at once

took us into his care. He set off up the glacier with the Satpora coolies to carry down George Bell and to help the others. That evening we were all together again and were able to talk of our experiences during the last days. We were slowly able to fit together the details of the fall and of our night at Camp VII. Until then, none of us was really sure what had happened.

K2: The cairn built by surviving expedition members in memory of Art Gilkey, just above where the Godwin-Austen and Savoia glaciers join.

Courtesy of the Streather family.

"Next morning we held a short memorial service for Art. The Colonel had built a splendid cairn on the spur of rock which juts out between the Godwin-Austen and Savoia glaciers. This was in a magnificent position

61

and could be seen from many miles away by anyone approaching the mountains. On this we left an aluminium box in which we had placed a few mountain flowers, a statement about Art's death and his favourite poem. His ice axe also lies there. After a short reading from the Bible we limped back to camp to prepare for our departure next day."

K2: On their return, expedition members meet General Ayub Khan, later President of Pakistan: (l-r) Peter Schoening, Bob Bates, Tony Streather, Charlie Houston, Gen Ayub Khan, Dee Molenar, Col Ata Ullah, Bob Craig. George Bell who was severely frostbitten did not attend the event.

Courtesy of Major-General Syed Ali Hamid.

The memorial is still there, with engraved tin plates and other items, tragically being added to on an annual basis. K2 is indeed a savage mountain.

Thus, Tony survived one of the most dramatic climbs of his career as a mountaineer. And indeed, one of the most dramatic and well-remembered climbs in the history of mountaineering. As Charlie Houston said: "*We went to the mountain as strangers and returned as brothers.*" Reinhold Messner said: "*They failed in the most beautiful way you can imagine.*" Theirs was an expedition where the humanity and brotherhood of men on a mountain came to the fore, and the glory of the summit was forgotten as all energies were redirected to try to save their colleague and themselves. The entire team was retrospectively awarded, in 1981, the David A. Sowles Memorial Award by the American Alpine Club for *"unselfish devotion to imperilled climbers"*. Tony returned to the US on many occasions for reunions invariably attended by all members of the expedition except for the greatly missed Art Gilkey and an absent Colonel Ata Ullah.

After K2, Tony returned to the Regiment at Warminster and then to Sandhurst as an instructor. However, this period of relative normality was not to last very long.

Kangchenjunga, the Untrodden Peak — 1955

In 1899, the explorer and mountaineer Douglas Freshfield described Kangchenjunga, third highest mountain in the world, straddling the Nepal-Sikkim border, in these terms: [14] *"The whole face of the mountain might be imagined to have been constructed by the Demon of Kangchenjunga for the express purpose of defence against human assault, so skilfully is each comparatively weak spot raked by the ice and snow batteries."* But he also saw a possible line of weakness: *"...the rock wall at the head of the Yalung Glacier might be overcome by the help of a shelf conspicuous to the right of a horseshoe cliff ... The western ridge would be gained close to the foot of the final peak and not far below it."*

In 1953 Charles Evans and George Band received the support of the Alpine Club to mount a strong reconnaissance expedition to Kangchenjunga.[15] Their task was to examine the upper part of the mountain, with the limited objective of reaching the Great Shelf, the ice terrace that Freshfield had noticed, stretching across the south west (Yalung) face at about 24,000 feet. At the same time, just in case things proved easier than expected, Evans was planning to take oxygen and sufficient equipment to launch an attack on the summit. This was to be a reconnaissance in force.

Evans's team comprised George Band, who had been with him on the 1953 Everest expedition, Norman Hardie, an experienced New Zealander, Joe Brown, one of the great rock climbers of his time but thus far without Himalayan experience, John Clegg, the team doctor, strong alpinists Neil Mather, John Jackson and Tom McKinnon, and

---

[14] Douglas W Freshfield, 1903, *Round Kangchenjunga*, Edward Arnold, London.
[15] Charles Evans, 1956, *Kangchenjunga – the Untrodden Peak*, Hodder and Stoughton, London.

last but not least Tony. Despite the emotional trauma of K2, Tony Streather had no qualms two years later when he was invited out of the blue by Charles Evans to go to Kangchenjunga. He would later comment: *"Charles was a terrific leader in a very quiet sort of way and, like K2, we all became great chums and a close team."*

Tony near the summit of Kangchenjunga.
Courtesy of the Streather family.

A lecture, illustrated with lantern slides, given by Tony at a joint meeting of the East India Association, the Pakistan Society and the Overseas League in October 1955, a few months after the expedition returned home, describes the adventure well, besides giving us a glimpse of Tony himself in more informal mood:[16]*"Kanchenjunga is*

---

[16] Captain H R A Streather, 1956, *The Ascent of Kanchenjunga*, Asian Review, vol. LII: 52-64.

very different from Everest, the highest mountain as we all know, and K2, the second highest mountain. Kanchenjunga is the third highest, and you can see it from Darjeeling. Everest and K2 are tucked away in the remote parts of the Himalayas or the Karakoram, and you cannot see them unless you are prepared to walk for possibly two weeks through very rough terrain. So there are few who have had the chance of seeing Everest or K2. There must be many who have been on leave to Darjeeling, who have lived in Darjeeling, or who have gone up there in the summer from the heat of Calcutta and have looked north at that wonderful view of Kanchenjunga. And in the Planters' Club, as many of you will know, there is a telescope on the lawn and many a person has sat looking through the telescope at Kanchenjunga and saying 'Of course, it will never be climbed.'"

Evans assembled his team and transport in Darjeeling in March 1955 and started the long approach march through East Nepal. But a problem soon arose as Tony describes: *"After a day or two, when we had sorted out our loads ... we heard that the people of Sikkim, which is a small, semi-autonomous state to the east of Nepal, were very worried about our climbing Kanchenjunga. We had not in any way applied to them for permission because we were going through Nepal, and the Nepalese Government had granted us permission to go through and try the mountain from their side. We were not going into Sikkim and so had not, in fact, approached them. When they heard of our coming, they had objected to the Indian Government and that got through to us through our High Commissioner, and we learnt then that they look upon Kanchenjunga as being a sacred mountain. As you know, they are all Buddhists, and they consider that the mountain is the home of some of their gods. The word Kanchenjunga, in fact, in Tibetan, means "The Five Sacred Treasures of the Snow." We were still not sure whether, in fact, when we got to Darjeeling, we would be able to go to the mountain we had come to climb. So Charles Evans, our leader, went down to Gangtok, the capital of Sikkim, to talk with the Raj Kumar, the Maharajah's son ... and after a long discussion they came to an agreement whereby, having come so far and made all our plans, we could still go to the mountain, but we would only go as far as was necessary to ensure that there was a route to the summit, and, if we found a feasible route, then in any case we would not violate the actual summit. That seemed a very happy agreement and so we set off, knowing that whatever happened we would not, in fact, tread on the very summit of Kanchenjunga."*

Tony's observations ranged far and wide. Here he is, talking about food, always a topic of obsessive interest for expedition members: *"People often ask what one eats on these expeditions and I remember particularly a story from Camp 2. We took all the essentials, but we also asked everyone what they particularly liked so they could have their particular fads. When you get high your appetite rather goes, and you don't feel much like eating, and then when you do feel like eating you feel like rather peculiar things. At Camp 2 Joe Brown made history, shall we say, by telling us about a meal he once had — half a pound of Cheddar cheese, half a bottle of tomato ketchup and half a Mars bar ..."*

With the expedition arrived at base camp under the Yalung Face, the first attempt to find a safe route to the great shelf failed, the icefall proving too long and far too dangerous. So base camp was laboriously moved to the site of an early attempt dating from 1909 and a way was eventually found over the top of the icefall. Then, in traditional style, a series of camps was slowly established and stocked, culminating in Camp 6 at 26,900 feet hewn out of a steep snow slope leading to the summit ridge.

Oxygen apparatus used on Kangchenjunga in 1955.
This only remaining apparatus can be found in the basement of the
Alpine Club's headquarters in Charlotte Road, London.

Courtesy of the Alpine Club.

The first summit pair were George Band and Joe Brown. From Camp 6, they continued steeply up to the summit ridge, following one false trail which lost them an hour and a half. By mid-afternoon with little oxygen left, they sensed they were near. George Band described the next moments:[17] *"There above us the wall was broken by several*

---

[17] George Band, 1955-56, *Kangchenjunga Climbed*, The Himalayan Journal, vol. XIX: 33-56, also Alpine Journal, vol. LX, no. 291: 207-226.

vertical cracks about twenty feet high, with a slight overhang to finish. Turning his oxygen to the full six litres a minute and safeguarding his lead with a couple of running belays, he [Joe] struggled and forced his way up. It was the hardest part of the whole climb; perhaps 'very difficult' had it been at normal altitudes. From the top, I remember him shouting, 'George, we're there!'

Tony Streather and Norman Hardie after their successful ascent of Kangchenjunga.

Courtesy of the Royal Geographical Society.

"I joined him, with no more than a tight rope I'm glad to say, and there before us, some twenty feet away and five feet higher than the ground on which we stood, was the very top, formed by a gently sloping cone of snow. It was a quarter to three. We had come as far as we were allowed."

Meanwhile, the second summit pair of Hardie and Streather had been climbing up to Camp 6 to try their luck the following day. They were anxiously awaiting the return of Brown and Band. Tony takes up the story: *"As the sun set behind Jannu it was getting rapidly dark and about then we heard bits of snow being kicked on to our tent and realised there was movement about. We went outside and shouted and there at last were the first pair! It was about 7 o'clock when the two very exhausted climbers came into view round the buttress of rock and flopped down exhausted on the little bit of level ice and snow in front of our tent. We heard from them the very great news that they had been to the near summit. There was no time for excitement because we realised now that, whatever happened, the four of us would have to spend a very uncomfortable night in that tiny tent, and we knew that the first pair were very exhausted; one of them, George Band, had slightly frost-bitten fingers where he had handled one of his oxygen cylinders without gloves on. Joe Brown had taken his goggles off for a short time to be able to see better on a difficult bit of rock and was slightly snow blind. We had to get them in, feed them up and give them plenty of liquid. At that altitude one needs a tremendous amount of liquid. You breathe in very dry air, and breathe out very moist air, and you lose something like six or seven pints of liquid a day just from breathing. Having given them gallons of tea and revived them a bit, we were able to hear their story. When we heard about the final rock pitch, Hardie and I thought 'We'll never make that'.*

"The next morning ... after they (Brown and Band) had gone down, Hardie and I set about preparing our own oxygen apparatus, ready for our own bid for the summit ... After we had been climbing for some time we passed the oxygen frames of the first party dumped on the rocks. They had left them there on their way down the day before, when their oxygen had run out. We had our first mishap just before this when one of the oxygen cylinders out of Hardie's frame had slipped from its straps and

gone falling down the mountain, banging on a rock, breaking open and hissing off down the mountain side. So we were now faced with having to make the summit climb, if we were still going to do it, with a very limited amount of oxygen. But we pushed on up and got on to the ridge, using now a very low flow rate of oxygen. Soon we came to the rock buttress near the summit, which we had heard so much about and which Joe Brown had climbed the day before. We looked up and did not like the look of it at all, so Hardie and I thought we would just have a look round the corner. We went round five or ten yards and there, sure enough, was a perfect little snow ridge running up to the summit. We reached a point near the summit just below a pyramid of snow. Fifteen feet away from us and five or six feet above was the actual summit of the mountain; and that was the part which was left untrodden. After a while on the summit, changing our oxygen cylinders and changing the films in our cameras, eating a few biscuits, chocolate, sweets, Kendal mint cake, we set out to come down again. By now Hardie had little oxygen left and I was out of it and had to come down all the way without, and found, in fact, the descent far worse than the ascent.

"We were met at Camp 5 by Charles Evans, who was waiting there in support, and as we drew near to it he shouted out 'Have you been to the top?' We thought a bit, thought it was rather a stupid question, because we could not think where else we had been all that time, so we did not trouble to answer. It was the 26th May. Hardie thought this one up. I am not quite sure how he did it in his rather muzzy state — he said: 'Charles, who won the Election?' Charles obviously thought that was a stupid question too and he did not answer. We joined him at Camp 5, rested there, and then went on down to Base Camp; but while we were at Camp 5 we heard from Charles the very sad news that one of our Sherpas had died in Base Camp at almost the exact time that we reached *the summit. He had been ill for a few days, and of course the Sherpas, who are in some ways superstitious, were saying that the Gods of Kanchenjunga had not let us get away with it scot-free after all. He was buried under a rock at Base Camp and the Sherpas carved on it the eternal Buddhist prayer:* Om Mane Padme Hum — Hail to the Jewel in the Lotus.*"*

Thus ended perhaps Tony's greatest mountaineering achievement. As with the previous two expeditions, deep friendships had been forged. Tony and the rest of the team enjoyed many reunions, at the Pen y Gwryd hotel in Snowdonia, in Nepal, and elsewhere.

Tony Streather, Neil Mather and George Band presented with silk scarves by Tenzin Norgay after returning from Kangchenjunga.

Alpine Club Photo Library, London.

Haramosh — 1957

On return from Kangchenchunga, Tony met Sue Huggan — he was best man at a friend's wedding where she was maid of honour — and they married in April 1956 with a honeymoon spent skiing at Chamonix. Their first child, Charlie, was born the following year, and it says a lot about Sue that in spite of their growing family she always supported Tony's periodic need to head for the mountains. And an opportunity soon appeared.

Tony, Sue and Charlie, 1957
Courtesy of the Streather family.

It was after lecturing on K2 in Oxford, two years later, that the Oxford University Mountaineering Club collared Tony with a proposition: *"They got me into a bar, plied me with several whiskies, then approached me to ask if I would lead their expedition to Haramosh. The Himalayan Committee would only give them the necessary support on condition that they had an older more experienced leader. I suppose they got me at a vulnerable moment and I said 'Yes, fine.' I was not long since married, with a very small child, and I should probably never have done it. Very irresponsible. But it was not long since I had left Pakistan and it was very tempting to go back and see old friends."*

Thus wrote Stephen Venables, the first British climber to scale Mt Everest without supplementary oxygen.[18] In a 2007 Sunday Times article based on an interview with Tony, Venables offers a succinct account of the tragedy that would unfold on this treacherous mountain. Ralph Barker's classic account *The Last Blue Mountain*[19] offers the definitive and gripping account, but we continue with Venables: *"And so the Streathers' army bungalow in Camberley, grandly named Barossa Farm, became expedition headquarters, visited each weekend by the four student members of the expedition. Wrapping supplies in old pages of the Telegraph, the forestry graduate from New Zealand, Rae Culbert, joked about the lack of more liberal reading matter. Easy-going, thoughtful and generous, he seems to have been liked by everyone. John Emery, who had delayed his medical finals at St*

---

[18] Stephen Venables, 2nd September 2007, *The Friends Who Died at the Top of the World*, The Sunday Times, London.

[19] Ralph Barker, 1959, *The Last Blue Mountain*, Chatto and Windus, London. A film showing a re-enactment of the Haramosh tragedy based on Ralph Barker's book was made jointly by the BBC and the Australian Broadcasting Commission. It can be viewed on YouTube by searching the title "He who dares. The last blue mountain Tony Streather".

Mary's Hospital in London to join the expedition, was quieter — Streather took to him immediately. His relationship with the American, Scott Hamilton, who raised much-needed funds from the US, was more nuanced; Hamilton proved somewhat out of his depth on the mountain. And he had an awkward relationship with the grammar school boy from Huddersfield who had instigated the whole project, Bernard Jillott. 'Bernard was the driving force – very ambitious, very efficient, very busy. Everything he had done, he had always finished at the top. Without being snobbish, he was from a working-class background. I got on with him alright, but I think he found me a bit conventional.'

"*One can understand all too easily the frustration of this talented young Yorkshireman forced to act as deputy to the moustachioed officer with the plummy voice. But the friction wasn't just about class, as Streather explains. 'I tried to share the leadership as much as possible, but he was very impulsive. And that was dangerous because his decision-making could be influenced by that impulsiveness.'*

"*Haramosh was a very ambitious target for the Oxford University Mountaineering Club. Rising to 24,270 feet in the Karakoram range of northern Pakistan, the virgin peak was unlikely to succumb to four young students, however determined. On 3rd August 1957, the five men had reached base camp in the Mani valley, a few days' journey from Pakistan's northern outpost of Gilgit. Looking up from their grassy meadow at the summit of Haramosh, 12,000 feet above them, it was immediately obvious that any attempt direct on the gigantic north face would be suicidal. Instead, with the help of five local men from the Hunza valley, they worked their way up a long flanking movement, thwarted by frequent heavy snowfalls. Often the men were confined to camp. On one such day, confined by the weather, Streather wrote in his diary, "Spent most of the afternoon reading. I thought a lot about Sue and the baby and missed them even more than usual."*

Haramosh: Tony performing his well-honed skills as baggage man.
Courtesy of the Streather family.

"On 21st August he noted, 'storm all day'. On the 26th, he noted, 'Weather bad all day. Found Bernard particularly trying.' On 9th September, he wrote, 'Terrible night. Tents completely buried. Not much *food now. Bernard completely ineffective.' Then the weather finally improved.*

"On the night of 14th September, Culbert, Emery, Jillott and Streather slept at Camp 4, at 20,000 feet, ready to explore the next step. Hamilton had agreed to wait down at Camp 3, until they returned from their reconnaissance. The following morning the Camp 4 team got away at 11.00 am and by three o'clock that afternoon they had reached their high point of 21,000 feet, rewarded by the kind of dazzling vistas which make all the backbreaking toil seem worthwhile. But they could see the huge gulf still separating them from the summit. Streather was adamant that it was time to turn back. And that would have been that — a commendable accident-free reconnaissance. But twenty-three year old Bernard Jillott demanded to carry on a little bit further, just to see over the next crest.

Haramosh: (l-r) Shakoor Beg, John Emery, Tony Streather, Rae Culbert.

Courtesy of the Streather family.

"Streather agreed reluctantly, staying with Rae Culbert while Jillott ploughed ahead, roped to medical student Emery. Jillott led forcefully, kicking steps in deep soft snow, keeping well clear of the treacherous cornice — an overhang of windblown snow, bulging out over the huge precipice on the left. To the right the slope curved out of sight, disappearing 8,000 feet down the immense north face of Haramosh. It seemed an innocuous enough slope until the two men suddenly, inexplicably, crumpled over.

"Watching a bizarre puppet dance of waving arms and legs, Streather thought for a moment that Jillott and Emery were larking about. Then he realised that the whole surface was moving, taking the two men down the convex slope. They disappeared. There was a moment of silence, then a loud roar as the avalanche erupted over an ice cliff, flinging them down the 8,000-foot wall.

Once they had recovered from the first terrible shock, Streather and Culbert climbed a short way down the convex slope, now swept clear to old frozen snow. It was really just a token gesture, a formality, but as they peered down the precipice they were astounded to see first one, then another tiny figure emerge from a pile of snow and stand up. Jillott and Emery had halted miraculously on a ledge.

Against all the odds, they were alive, but they were stranded without food, water or shelter in a remote snow basin, possibly injured, one thousand feet below the ridge. Streather and Culbert knew immediately that they had to go down into that basin and rescue their companions. What they didn't know was that the accident they had just witnessed was merely the prelude to a tale of compounding misfortune, catastrophe and heroic sacrifice almost unparalleled in the history of mountaineering.

"Streather and Culbert had to act fast. First they threw down a rucksack with warm down jackets and food, but it shot past the two men below and disappeared into a crevasse. However, there were more *supplies down at Camp 4, so they returned there to collect two thermos flasks, food, warm clothing and rope.*

Traversing the lower slopes of Haramosh.
Courtesy of the Streather family.

"*Then they climbed back up the route which had taken them four hours that morning. By the time they were back at the accident site it was already dark, but with the help of a good moon, they began climbing down into the snow basin. By this time another day had dawned, and Emery and Jillott were shouting urgently to them to avoid the huge ice cliff they had been swept over and traverse several hundred feet right, to a point where the cliff petered out. The traverse was steep, with thin snow overlaying brittle ice. Streather had to cut steps with his axe all the way, foot by foot. Towards the end of the traverse one of Culbert's crampons fell off and disappeared into the void. It was late afternoon by the time they reached Emery and Jillott.*

"*Although it was getting dark, Streather decided that they should start to climb out of the basin straight away, that evening. He led the way, bringing the others up on the rope, but Culbert slipped on his cramponless left foot and pulled them all back into the basin. They tried again, but this time Jillott fell asleep on a ledge and pulled them all off again, tumbling back into the basin, where they all spent another night in the open.*

"*They tried again on the 16th and this time all four men succeeded, despite exhaustion and frostbite, in climbing up the initial slope and across the laborious traverse. But traversing on ice is very hard, especially if on one foot all you have is the rubber sole of your frozen leather boot. Culbert tried heroically but eventually came off, swinging in a huge pendulum and ripping Streather from the ice and hurtling back down the same cliff over which Emery and Jillott had tumbled two days earlier. As if in some horrible cosmic joke, roles had been reversed, and the rescuers had now become the victims.*

"*While Emery and Jillott continued through the night, climbing back up to the ridge, Streather and Culbert shivered through another night in the basin. By the morning of the 17th Culbert was very weak and so frostbitten that he had lost all sensation in his feet. Streather had lost his ice axe, so knew he couldn't possibly hold the younger man, so they didn't bother to rope up as they set off out of the basin for the fourth time. Culbert tried to follow but kept sliding back down. He never complained, but just shouted up, 'What shall we do?' Streather shouted back, 'Hang on where you are. The others are sure to be back soon.' But the others failed to appear, so Streather just had to keep climbing on his own. Having lost his ice axe, he had to scoop powder snow with his frozen canvas mitten from the steps he had cut two days earlier, teetering across the traverse, until he finally regained the ice axe where he had fallen the previous afternoon. Even with his ice axe, the final slope back to the ridge was purgatory.*

"*Recalling it fifty years on, he said, 'I thought I was dead and I didn't know why I was climbing, but I just knew I had to keep moving, for Sue and the baby. I had this incredible feeling that someone was helping me, pulling me out of a well. And eventually I reached the ridge, where we had left a rucksack. I scooped up some glucose tablets with my frozen hands and mushed them up with some ice, then carried on down to Camp 4, as there was no sign of the others.'*

"The route down to the camp was complicated and at one point the tracks went straight over an open crevasse. Streather just managed to throw himself over. Lower down he was puzzled by one track diverging to the right, but he followed the correct route to the camp, where he found Emery lying, fully clothed, with his cramponed feet sticking out of the tent. When Streather asked where Jillott was, Emery blurted, 'He's gone.' 'What do you mean – gone?' asked Streather. 'He's dead. Over the edge.'

"Streather immediately understood the diverging track. Racing down in the dark, desperate to reach camp, Jillott had strayed over a

precipice, to fall several thousand feet down the south side of the mountain. Meanwhile Emery had fallen in a crevasse and only escaped that morning, reaching camp just a few hours before Streather.

Haramosh: Bernard Jillot and John Emery, seconds before being caught in an avalanche that carried them 1000 feet down to a snow basin to the right.

Courtesy of the Streather family.

"Streather got the stove going, to melt pan after pan of snow, desperate for liquid. Emery, the doctor, gave them both penicillin jabs to protect frostbitten hands and feet from infection. And they talked about going back to rescue Rae Culbert. But the following morning they realised it was impossible."

Tony and John Emery descending after the final rescue attempts. Photo taken by Scott Hamilton.

Courtesy of the Streather family.

Fifty years on Streather was still wracked by regret. *"I tried getting out of the tent, but I couldn't even stand up. In the end I had to use ski sticks. John was even weaker and I realised that we were incapable of going back. In any case, Rae was almost certainly dead already, after another night in the open. If we had gone back, probably no one would have survived. As it was, we had a terrible struggle getting down to Camp 3 and when we got there, Scott Hamilton was too shocked to be any use.*

We had to make all the decisions and do everything ourselves. It took them four days to get down to base, before they could send telegrams home to the families of Bernard Jillott and Rae Culbert."

Back at St Mary's Hospital in London, John Emery had to have all his fingers and toes amputated. But the surgeons left enough of a thumb and first finger stump for him to hold a pen and get a First in his medical Finals. Emery subsequently recuperated with the Streathers, and Tony's wife Sue spent months dressing his wounds. Soon he was climbing again, but in 1963 he died in a fall in the Alps. He was descending the Weisshorn with an American climbing friend, David Sowles, when they were caught in an electrical storm.

Streather got away without major amputations, just the ends of his big toes. But he still had to face the families of the young men who had died. *"The Jillotts didn't want to have anything to do with us, and that was very hard. But with the Culberts it was very different and I'm still in touch with Rae's brother Bill — very artistic chap, who was studying at the Royal College of Art."* Bill was to become godfather along with John Emery to Tony and Sue's second son, Peter, born in 1958.

Inevitably, Streather still wonders whether the whole disaster could have been averted. *"Perhaps if I had been stronger, I could have stopped Bernard going up that last slope. But he was determined, and I couldn't physically stop him."*

It is perhaps a sign of the trauma experienced by the survivors that no account of the expedition was published in the standard climbing literature. There was the briefest of mentions in the end pages of *The Himalayan Journal* and a short and rather dry summary attributed to Tony in the *American Alpine Journal*. This summary contains the extraordinary error of stating that Emery died while Culbert survived — presumably an editor failing to grasp the terrible irony of the rescue attempt. When Haramosh was successfully climbed by an Austrian team one year later, leader Heinrich Roiss remarked in his article in the 1958 edition of *The Himalayan Journal*:[20] "*At the time of our departure from Vienna ... I had not heard anything about Capt. Streather's attempt in 1957.*"

---

[20] H Roiss: *1958 Austrian Expedition: the Ascent of Haramosh*, The Himalayan Journal, vol. XXI: 60-77.

The Army Mountaineering Association

At about the time the Haramosh expedition was being planned, there was a move in the Army to capitalise on an already substantial record of mountaineering achievement and form a proper climbing club. The Army had been involved in many climbing initiatives from the early 1900s, including a strong involvement in the pre-Second World War expeditions to Everest. During the war, the British Army fielded a Division of Mountain Trained troops, and by 1957 the Army had mounted a number of successful expeditions around the world, including Lieutenant James Waller's and Lieutenant John Hunt's trip to climb K36 (Saltoro Kangri) in Baltistan. Lieutenant (later Colonel and Lord) Hunt would subsequently be appointed to lead the successful 1953 Everest expedition.

The prime movers in creating a club were Colonel Gerry Finch, Major Hugh Robertson and Second Lieutenant Chris Bonington. A plot was hatched in the Ministry of Supply in London in May 1957. Envisaged was a club with the strength to organise alpine meets and expeditions to the greater ranges, initiatives that Regimental clubs were unable to support. In 1957, a formal proposal was drawn up and accepted by the Army Sports Control Board, who were particularly receptive to the emphasis being placed on the training value of mountaineering. It was agreed to invite Field Marshal Gerald Templer to be President and Sir John Hunt as Vice-President; both accepted. Financial support — £100 up front and £150 annually — was agreed subject to 'the organisation being integrated as far as practicable with the Army Ski Association.' The link never materialised, and the Army Mountaineering Association — the AMA as it became known — remains independent to this day. Gerry Finch, never a man for rule by committee, took the Army Ski Association crest, changed the wording and substituted crossed ice axes for the crossed skis.

In an article that appeared in *Mountain Moments – a Miscellany Celebrating 40 Years of the Army Mountaineering Association*, Tony described his initial reaction to such an organisation:[21] "*Mountaineers are well known for being pretty independent-minded sort of people! When I was approached in late 1956, about the possibility of forming an Army-wide climbing club of some sort, I was not particularly enthusiastic. If people wanted to climb, they would get on with it without other people having to organise it for them.*" Later recanting, he wrote: "*I was busy preparing for Haramosh when I was approached about the Army climbing club and hence my lack of interest. On my return from Haramosh I found that the Committee had assumed that I would join in due course and had kindly kept a number for me as a Founder Member of The Army Mountaineering Association – no. 007. I have Colonel Gerry Finch, whose idea it was to form the Association, to thank for this.*"

Col Finch immediately proposed a first AMA expedition to the Himalayas and consulted the officer with the most Himalayan experience. Tony continues: "*I was asked for my ideas about this and was firmly of the opinion that the expedition should be so planned that new blood from the Army would be introduced to the Himalayas. The plan should allow for the maximum amount of travel and climbing by small parties within the expedition. There was little point in just collecting together the few Himalayan 'old hands' who were serving at that time, with the object of making a desperate attempt on the 'highest*

---

[21] Lt Col (retd) H R A Streather, *A Word from the President 007* in Lt Col (retd) A J Muston, 1997, *Mountain Moments – a Miscellany Celebrating 40 Years of the Army Mountaineering Association*, privately published.

unclimbed' or the 'most difficult' Himalayan peak.

"These ideas were accepted, and in due course I was invited to get on with it. I was not overly enthusiastic about this as I had hardly recovered from the traumatic time we had had on Haramosh, and I was meant to be studying for Staff College. (I never did get to the place!) My family too had been through enough already. However, the idea of a return to Pakistan was always attractive and I thought I had better make sure that I hadn't lost my nerve. Having forfeited some months of seniority, pay and service towards pension while away on K2, I insisted that we should be considered as on duty. This was eventually agreed and so the seeds for [paid] Adventure Training were sown. The area selected was that of the Tirich Gol in Chitral. This would have given access to the mass of glaciers and unclimbed peaks that lie along the Afghanistan border to the north of Tirich Mir. But at the eleventh hour we heard that political permission had not been granted so we went instead to the Chogo Lungma area to the north of Gilgit. This proved to be ideal for what we planned to do.

"Our stated aim was to introduce personnel with some background of mountaineering or expedition experience to mountaineering and travel in high Asiatic terrain, with a view to training a nucleus of instructors for organising expeditions in future years. It seems hard to believe now, but we had some difficulty in raising the numbers we required. Other than officers, we could find only one who qualified, Sergeant Mike Quinn, who at that time was an Instructor at the Army Outward Bound School at Tywyn. There was Gwen Moffat, WRAC, an accomplished climber, but at that time having a female in the party was quite unthinkable as far as the War Office was concerned! Two officers from the Royal Navy joined us, as did three from the Pakistan Army. Of these Captain Javed Akhtar went on to become one of Pakistan's most distinguished mountaineers. Sadly he was killed in the Bangladesh war.

The Pakistan Army helped in every possible way and their Commander-in-Chief, Field Marshal Ayub Khan [later President of Pakistan] became one of our Patrons.

*AMA expedition: Gloster peak with Tony in foreground.
The expedition named the peak after their regiment, simply for temporary identification, but the name stuck and has since appeared on maps.
Expedition members made the first ascent.*

Courtesy of the Streather family.

"We had a most successful expedition. We climbed six new peaks between 17,000 and 23,000 feet, including the first ascent of Malubiting East, and Gloster and Engineers Peaks, both over 19,000 feet. These names were purely for our own identification, but they seem to have found their way onto the Karakoram map! We also visited several new passes on the Hispar Wall."

On the Haramosh La: (l-r) Doctor Philip Horniblow, Major P G H Varwell*, Captain Jowed (Pakistan Army), Second Lieutenant H G F Chapman*, Captain H R A Streather*. Asterisks indicate the Gloucestershire Regiment. The cairn was erected by a German expedition in 1955.

Courtesy of Lt Col (retd) Robert Dixon.

The expedition fielded two doctors; one was Philip Horniblow, Special Air Services (retd.). In his book *Oil, Sand and Politics*, Horniblow mentions an event that does not appear in any account Tony would have given of the expedition.[22] One night, when they were sharing a tent, Horniblow recounts: *"The night was disturbed. I was awakened in the early morning by strangled cries and by the light of my torch saw Tony clawing up the tent wall. I called out 'Tony! Wake up!' He did so, fighting for breath and gasped that he had dreamed he was back on Haramosh. Later he apologised for disturbing my sleep!"*

---

[22] Philip Horniblow, 2004, *Oil, Sand & Politics: Memoirs of a Middle East Doctor, Mercenary & Mountaineer*, Hayloft Publishing, Kirby Stephen.

With the expedition objectives achieved, Tony decided to return via Gilgit rather than Skardu, using a direct route over the Haramosh La and taking with him George Chapman, also of the Glosters. Following a heavy snowfall during the night, Horniblow and three others including deputy leader Fred Jenkins, an Army Chaplain, accompanied Tony and Chapman to the top of the Haramosh La, where, as Horniblow describes, *"We built two cairns in memory of Bernard Jillott and New Zealander Rae Culbert who had died on the mountain two years previously. Fred led us in prayer for their souls which reduced Tony to tears. For those of us who had read* The Last Blue Mountain, *this was hardly surprising. I cannot think of an epic save Shackleton's escape to South Georgia from the Antarctic ice, to equal it."* Tony and George Chapman then began a long descent down the Mani valley, a route close to that followed by Tony and John Emery after the Haramosh epic. On the way down Tony met old friends who had helped at that time and welcomed the opportunity to thank them again. In Gilgit he arranged for a plaque to be fixed in memory of the two Haramosh climbers.

The AMA subsequently prospered, but climbing activity gradually became more focused on the UK and the Alps rather than the far-off Himalayas. This all changed in late 1966 as Tony recalled: *"Well do I remember our Annual General Meeting of December 1966, held in a scruffy little room in the old War Office building. Our first President, Field Marshal Templer was present. It was then four years since any of our members had organised a major expedition. This had been to Khinyang Chhish (25,760 feet) in the Karakoram. Tragically Jimmy Mills, the leader, and Dick Jones were killed in an avalanche and so we lost two of our most prominent and active mountaineers. There was much talk at the meeting about various minor matters and particularly of the possibility of acquiring a hut in North Wales. Clearly the Field Marshal was becoming irritated and eventually, in his well-known forthright manner, he said 'To hell with huts in Wales, what about getting on with some expeditions', or words to that effect! With that he walked out, so ending his time as President. Brigadier Sir John Hunt, then AMA Vice President, replaced him. We should be grateful to the Field Marshal, because his comments kick-started a series of expeditions that were to follow — Greenland in 1967 and 1968, Tirich Mir in 1969, Annapurna in 1970 through to Nuptse, Everest and Gasherbrum ..."*

Tony would eventually become President of the AMA, as the organisation embraced all types of mountaineering from Himalayan expeditions to bouldering, rock climbing, sports climbing competitions and alpine expeditions. From Colonel Finch as member 002 through to Corporal Beasley at no. 5000, the membership has gone from strength to strength. There is no longer any problem finding climbers fit for a serious expedition; rather, there's an embarrassment of riches from the many hundreds who are perfectly well qualified.

The Soldiering Life

In 1981 when Tony was obliged to retire from the Army, he put together a Curriculum Vitae, perhaps with a view to seeking further employment. It provides a key reference in following the full span of his 40-year military career, particularly the non-mountaineering or plain soldiering part of his life. It starts with his service on the Indian subcontinent and quickly catalogues those famous mountaineering expeditions:

SERVICE CAREER AND EXPERIENCE

1944	*Joined in the ranks during the War following service in the Home Guard.*
	Sailed for India for officer training.
1945-50	*Commissioned into the Indian Army.*
	Active Service on North-West Frontier with local Troops; speaking only Pushtu and Urdu.
	Tour as ADC to Governor of North-West Frontier Provinces involving work with all senior politicians and serving officers in Pakistan and India.
	Service as last British Officer in Chitral on the Russian-Chinese border. Exploration and travel in remote mountain regions.
	Member of Norwegian Expedition and in summit party to be first to climb Tirich Mir - 25,263 feet
	Elected to Alpine Club and to be Fellow of Royal Geographical Society.
1951-55	*Returned from Pakistan and joined 1st Bn The Gloucestershire Regiment in Korea. Active service in Korea.*

> *Remained with Battalion in various junior staff and command appointments until 1955.*
>
> *During this time was member of American Expedition to K2, 28,250 ft, the world's second highest mountain and in summit team of British Expedition which was first to climb Kangchenjunga, 28,146 ft, the world's third highest mountain in 1955. Much involved with planning and organisation of these two major expeditions as well as normal military duties.*
>
> *Able to make use of knowledge of languages in dealing with local people.*

Languages again! The ability to learn local languages and dialects in India and Pakistan, as noted above, was remarkable for a boy who claimed to have been no scholar at school. The CV records his speaking Pushtu, Urdu, Gurkhali and Malay, but also records that he could get by in numerous dialects from the North-West Frontier region where each valley had its own patois. Yet when he and his wife Sue bought a house in Brittany where they spent holidays with their friends, the Matsons, Tony never mastered the French language.

In 1951 when Tony ended his time with the Chitral Scouts and returned to the UK, his first duty involved taking a first draft of men to Korea to help reform the Glosters after their heroic stand against overwhelming Chinese forces at the Battle of the Imjin River. The Regimental History refers to him as '*Lt Streather*', so he must have reverted to his substantive rank having been a Captain in the Pakistan Army. There was an amusing upside, nevertheless. He was awarded a medal by Pakistan, when the country was still a Dominion with Queen Elizabeth II as head of state. His Pakistan medal with the Queen's head on it would be placed chronologically in the middle of his row of medals where it belonged. This did not please one Adjutant of the day who ordered him to put it at the end of his row of medals because it was 'foreign'. Tony did as he was told until the Adjutant was out of sight and then returned it to its original position. This was repeated so often that the offending medal became known in the Glosters as 'Tony's middle medal'.

Four years later we find him at Sandhurst:

1955-58 *Instructor at Royal Military Academy, Sandhurst. Teaching all usual military subjects as well as military history.*
Responsible for extramural activities including mountaineering and exploration as well as riding.
During this period led Oxford University Expedition to Haramosh in 1957.
Lectured extensively in UK and also in Norway and America on previous expeditions.
Founder member Army Mountaineering Association in 1957.

By this time, and unstated in his CV, Tony had acquired international renown in climbing circles, with memberships of the Alpine Club, the Appalachian Mountain Club in the USA and honorary membership of the Norwegian Alpine Club. It was undoubtedly in character, but he probably downplayed his mountain fame in case the Army bosses thought he was losing interest in soldiering. However, as the CV will unfold, there is no disguising the fact that he managed to slot mountains and adventure quite liberally within the confines of his military duties. The Streather family was also growing. Charles had been born just before Haramosh. During the next six years, he was joined by siblings Peter, Phil and Sally.

1959-1962 *Organised and led first Army Mountaineering Association Expedition to Karakoram.*
Returned to 1st Battalion Gloucestershire Regiment as Company Commander and Adjutant in BAOR.
Posted as Chief Instructor, Army Outward Bound School [Tywyn], North Wales.
Gaining considerable interest in character development of young people
through adventure.
Elected to committee of Alpine Club.
Helped Sir John Hunt on a Duke of Edinburgh's Award expedition for young people to Greenland and acted as his deputy on a similar expedition to the Pindus mountains of Greece.

On his return from the successful AMA expedition to the Karakoram, Tony was posted as a Company Commander and subsequently Adjutant of the 1st Battalion of the Glosters as part of the British Army of the Rhine (BAOR) and stationed at Osnabrück Garrison, near the city of the same name. The position of Adjutant in an infantry regiment was usually held by a young Captain awaiting Staff College, but Tony was by now a Major, aged 34. The anomalous posting was perhaps typical for the era, as the British Army was in a state of flux. Beginning in 1960, a predominantly national service organisation — only a quarter of the armed forces were volunteers — was transforming itself into a purely professional Army. The shrinkage of personnel created less opportunity for career officers. And Tony's career had not been exactly typical. He had come from the Indian Army, commanded a thousand men at the age of 20, and arguably spent as much time climbing mountains as soldiering. Still, serving as an Adjutant was an essential step to being considered for the command of a Regiment later on.

Less than a year later, the Glosters were repatriated to Dover. The normal repatriation procedure would have been to transport the Regiment by train from their base in Germany to the Hook of Holland, take the ferry to Harwich, and then have everyone travel by train via London to Dover. Tony went to work on his superiors and after much persuasion got the ferry diverted down the Channel and delivered 600 soldiers straight into the mouth of Dover harbour. Less impressive, however, were the living quarters that greeted them. Grandly placed in the neighbourhood of Dover Castle, the officers' accommodation passed muster, but the soldiers' married quarters turned out to be squalid and unliveable. Tony had the place condemned and moved his troops to a neighbouring garrison at Deal.

Dover hardly counted as a glamorous assignment with its routine soldiering, inspections by senior staff, make-believe exercises and the occasional visit by one's Royal Colonel, in the case of the Glosters, the aged Duke of Gloucester. Thankfully, relief from the humdrum soon arrived. Tony was called to take over the Army Outward Bound School at Tywyn in North Wales, then organise and lead the AMA Karakoram expedition of 1959, and finally help Sir John Hunt plan Duke of Edinburgh's Award expeditions. For a while it was back to the old life — that is until Cyprus intervened.

1962-64   *Rejoined Glosters as Company Commander in Cyprus. Awarded MBE for active service during racial riots between Greeks and Turks in 1963/4.*

> *Responsible for civil administration of large areas during troubles.*
>
> *Chairman of local riding and polo club.*
>
> *Became Chairman of the John Hunt Exploration Group of Endeavour Training.*

In 1963, the Battalion was dispatched to Cyprus as part of a UN peace-keeping force to control the increasing tension between the Greek and Turkish communities. Tony's handling of the confrontation, a tricky balance between not doing enough and doing too much, must have been sufficiently well judged to gain him an MBE. Tony left a remarkable account of his time in Cyprus:

"*In May 1963 I rejoined the Battalion in Cyprus. It so happened that the previous month I had taken part in an expedition that walked from the South to the North of Greece through the Pindus mountains. I was later to learn that most of the Greeks in Cyprus were very different from the tough, straightforward likeable people I met in the mountains of Greece ... For an Infantry Battalion, Cyprus at that time must have been one of the best possible stations. The climate was good, the countryside was attractive, sandy beaches were plentiful and the wine cheap. On the surface the people seemed cheerful and there was certainly no anti-British feeling. Our barracks in Episkopi were the best we had seen for years. We could train almost anywhere on the Island and we were left alone. One could ski in the Troodos mountains in the morning and swim at Episkopi Bay in the afternoon of the same day.*

"*It was against this background that trouble was steadily brewing and reports started to come in of increasing inter-communal tension ... As Christmas 1963 drew near, tension increased and we were put on short notice to move to protect the families in Limassol. Some days before Christmas one of my soldiers came and asked for a confidential word. He had been playing darts and drinking with some Greek friends the evening before and had overheard some very alarming remarks ... that an attack by the Greek Cypriots with their secret army against the Turks was imminent. I passed him on to the Intelligence Corps at HQ Cyprus.*

"*Fighting broke out on the other side of the island a couple of days before Christmas. During Christmas Day the festivities went on though we were on four hours' notice to move. At a party in my house in the evening, the CO was sent for by the General. An O (Orders) group was held in my hall ... we were to move later, on Boxing Day morning. The next morning we made a fine sight as we drove out of Episkopi with Union Jacks streaming from tent poles tied to our Land Rovers. As we approached 'Half Way House', a Turkish enclave ... crude blocks had been erected across the road. Turks with shot guns and sundry other weapons were manning the blocks. These were pulled aside as we approached and we were waved cheerfully through. But it was clear that no Greeks would pass that way today. As we skirted the city of Nicosia, we found the streets deserted and the houses shuttered. The few bewildered people hanging about the corners raised a pathetic cheer as we drove past, somehow thinking that their troubles were now over. Little did they know that they were just beginning.*

"*The politicians and General Young[23] tried to come to some form of Tripartite agreement for the deployment of the Truce Force which initially was to include both Greek and Turkish battalions. Mutual mistrust and fear made this impossible and so for three difficult months peace-keeping duties were carried out exclusively by British troops.*

"*The scene in Nicosia was grim. A number of corpses still littered the streets. Looting and vandalism had been horribly thorough. Whole rows*

---

[23] Major General Peter Young was the commander of the British Joint Force (later known as the Truce Force and a predecessor of the present UN force).

of houses had been disgustingly ransacked and a wave of uncontrollable arson was rapidly spreading. It was at this stage that the 'Green Line' agreement was reached. That was the colour of the chinagraph pencil the General happened to have in his hand at the time.

"We were to move in and take over from the Greek and Turkish positions on this 'frontier'. Mine was the first company in and my positions were Company HQ in the Ledra Palace hotel and the other platoons were to be in the Conaro Hotel, the Nicosia Club and the Residency. Never again will I occupy such luxurious positions. I later received a bill for over £500 for rent of the Ledra Palace ballroom where my soldiers slept on camp beds and the General was sent a bill for £60,000 for forceful entry into the Conaro Hotel.

"Having established our company positions, there then came the task of clearing armed Greek and Turkish people back to their respective sides behind the Green Line and then ensuring that they kept back. It was here the patience and tact of the British soldier came into its own."

Tony's approach was always jaw-jaw rather than war-war. This philosophy had worked well with reluctant porters in the North-West Frontier, and it worked with the Greeks and Turks of Cyprus.

"Back in Nicosia we were again on the Green Line in the northern suburbs where the situation was particularly tense. Both sides were rapidly becoming frustrated by the lack of any apparent progress towards reaching a political agreement. Both sides were now better organised and bursting for a fight. The Greeks were impatient to get stuck into the Turks again. The Turks would have welcomed this and provoked the Greeks in every way they could, because they were confident now that another serious outbreak of fighting would lead to intervention by Turkey who had a large force poised just over the water.

"Our positions were so sited that we could fire along the Green Line

... How we should do this in self-defence was never quite established. My main contact on the Greek side was a fanatical Police Sergeant called Bambos. I used to have to spend hours drinking coffee with him in his temporary Police Station ... so that I could keep tags on him (even Greeks drink Turkish coffee). It was not unusual for him to summon a few of his 'Special Police' (would be EOKA[24] thugs), jump into his Land Rover and race off down to the Green Line. Within minutes he would have been met by Turkish Cypriot police and both sides would face each other across the road with cocked rifles shouting abuse and provoking each other all they could. One shot from an excited youth on these occasions could have led to terrible consequences.

"*I think the nearest anyone came to firing during this period was when the Greek police were incensed by Turkish shepherds who drove their sheep into the wheat fields which the Greeks claimed were theirs, on either side of the Green Line. At one stage a young policeman jumped into a trench, took careful aim at a Turkish shepherd and I swear was about to press the trigger when he received a smart whack on his bottom from my walking stick.[25] He failed to shoot the shepherd but turned round and threatened to shoot me!*"

The most serious incident took place in the Troodos foothills, when the Greeks launched a full-scale attack on the small isolated village of Malia: "*Hundreds of women and children took refuge in the school building at one end of the village. Even after the Turks surrendered their weapons, the Greeks opened fire on the school with rocket launchers. The commander of the Recce Platoon Detachment of the Glosters had no*

---

[24] EOKA was the acronym for a Greek Cypriot nationalist guerrilla organisation.

[25] Gloster officers always carried a regimental ash walking stick, rather than side arms or the like. There was even a drill that young officers had to learn when they first joined the Battalion on how to carry and use it.

option but to reply with the Browning machine gun of his Ferret Scout Car. There was a surprised silence and not another shot was fired. I moved in next day with my company HQ to try to sort out the refugee problem. It was impossible to remain impartial about Malia. This was out-and-out aggression by the Greeks, and the wanton destruction caused by them had to be seen to be believed. It was at this time that the Glosters fired their only shot in anger."

1963, Kenya: Rest and recreation for the Glosters during their peace-keeping role in Cyprus. Tony took a group of his soldiers to Mount Kilimanjaro, and seven made it to the top.

Courtesy of Lt Col (retd) Robert Dixon.

Tony made no bones about the difficulties the British troops experienced:

"Much of the time the task was dull and monotonous with endless hours

of patrolling and sentry duty with nothing to report. But there were flashes of danger and excitement. And always there was the acknowledgment that a faulty decision, a rude word at the wrong time, a sleepy sentry could lead to disastrous consequences."

There were, however, opportunities to switch off. Time was spent skiing or walking in the Troodos mountains, relaxing at Tunnel Beach and playing polo. The Regiment even found time to conduct a polo tour in nearby Jordan. And mountaineering was never far away. In the summer of 1963, Tony led twenty-two of his men on an Adventure Training Expedition to Kenya. Flown there from Cyprus by courtesy of the RAF, the first objective was Mount Kilimanjaro. Injuries and altitude sickness gradually reduced the party to eleven, and on the day of the final assault seven made it to the top — at 19,341 feet the highest point in Africa. Not a bad achievement for a bunch of first-timers led by one who himself had been a first-timer all those years ago. The following week they moved north to Mount Kenya where eleven made Point Lenana, the trekking summit, leaving Gloster cap badges in the box at the top.

In 1964, Tony left Cyprus and was seconded to serve in Malaysia, a federation of Malaya, Singapore, and the Borneo territories of Sabah and Sarawak formed the previous year:[26]

1964-66 *Posted to Malaya to help raise new Regiment for Malaysian Army.*
Learnt Malay and became an expert in Jungle Warfare.
Moved to Hong Kong to join Gurkhas.
Learnt Gurkhali and saw active service with

---

[26] Singapore was expelled from Malaysia in 1965.

> *them in Borneo during confrontation with Indonesia.*

The move started badly. Tony, his wife Sue and their family moved to Ipoh in northern Malaya, the home of the Malay Jungle Warfare Training Centre, where he was to be second-in-command of the 3rd Malay Rangers; a fellow Gloster officer was to be Adjutant of the 1st Malay Rangers. It will be remembered that Tony was trained in jungle warfare when he joined the Indian Army at the beginning of his career. Both had been given to understand that they would subsequently be promoted in their respective Malay Regiments. On arrival, however, they found that the War Office had already filled both posts and blithely forgotten to inform them, and presumably also their Regiment. Tony's wife Sue is reliably reported to have taken the senior officer responsible by the throat! A posting was subsequently found for Tony in the 1st Battalion of the 6th Gurkha Rifles in Hong Kong, meagre compensation for such administrative incompetence. Tony used the time to add Malay and Nepali to his already long list of languages. All this time, a festering insurgency on the island of Borneo was threatening to burst into the open.

Beginning in 1962, President Sukarno of Indonesia began interfering politically and militarily in the northern Borneo territories, perhaps with a view to securing the whole island for himself — Indonesia already claimed the vast southern part of the island, known as Kalimantan. His first target was Brunei, a tiny oil-rich enclave sandwiched between Sabah and Sarawak that had decided against joining the Malaysian federation. Sukarno's poorly equipped forces were easily repulsed. He then turned his attention to Sabah and Sarawak, infiltrating armed groups across the border through dense jungle in the hope of destabilising the young Malaysia.

It was a full-scale guerilla campaign, and Britain and several Commonwealth countries soon responded to young Malaysia's call for help, providing up to 30,000 troops including the Brigade of Gurkhas to which Tony was now attached. Combating the Indonesian incursions called for small troop detachments no larger than platoon or company strength. They were led by officers such as Tony, skilled in jungle warfare, and local tribesmen were recruited to act as the eyes and ears for the regular troops. At times, the fight against Sukarno called for clandestine cross-border operations — every such sortie had to be cleared by London. The so-called 'Confrontation' continued for four years, until Sukarno was ousted by political rivals.

At one point during the crisis, Tony was stationed in Brunei with his Gurkhas and got to know the Sultan. This may well explain how Tony managed to fit in the odd chukka of polo there, and why the Sultan was later persuaded to pay for the refurbishment of the Old Riding School at Sandhurst! Although seconded to the Gurkhas, the emotional ties to the Glosters and their glorious history and traditions remained strong. On one leave, while staying in a vast colonial, mock-Tudor hotel called the Smokehouse, in Malaysia's Cameron Highlands, he noticed that a silver candelabra in the dining room was in fact part of the Regimental silver, which had been hidden during the brutal Burmese campaign in the Second World War. Arranging for a replica to be made, he effected an exchange and had the original candelabra safely returned to regimental headquarters in the UK.

1967-70 *Commanded 1st Battalion in Berlin*
Moved Battalion to Northern Ireland

Succeeding to the command of one's Regiment is the greatest achievement of any military officer and for Tony this milestone occurred on 1st March 1967.[27] He wrote: *"I have always considered that to command one's Battalion should be the highlight of one's military career and I have always put my soldiers' welfare before my personal ambitions."*

1968, Berlin: Opening of the Corporals Club, aptly named the Gloucestershire Arms.

Courtesy of Lt Col (retd) Robert Dixon.

Berlin, his first posting as Commanding Officer, was not to Tony's liking. Military duties in Berlin, initially interesting, soon lost their

---

[27] Following the government's decision to reduce the size and number of infantry regiments in 1947, the 1st and 2nd Battalions of the Glosters were amalgamated at a parade held in Jamaica on 21st September 1948 which saw the birth of the 1st Battalion, the Gloucestershire Regiment (28th/61st).

appeal. There were crash training exercises in the middle of the night to meet the threat of a Russian invasion, code-named *Rocking Horse*, incessant border patrols, the rather weird necessity of guarding Rudolf Hess in Spandau Prison, to the utmost trivial such as finding a train guard for the daily run through East Germany to Helmstedt just across the border in West Germany. Compensations for Tony included the excellent horse-riding facilities and a swimming pool, inherited by the British courtesy of Hitler's Third Reich.

There were darker clouds on the horizon, however. As part of the general post-war reduction in the British Forces, Tony learned that the Glosters, a regiment with a proud and almost unbeaten record covering three hundred years' service, were to be amalgamated with the Royal Hampshire Regiment. On 11th July 1968, Tony had the Battalion formed up in a 'hollow square'[28], a battle formation that had served the Glosters so well in engagements from the Napoleonic Wars to Korea and announced to his troops the Government decision. A final ceremonial parade was held in Brooke Barracks in Berlin nine months later, meticulously planned by Tony. Whatever else he thought of the amalgamation of the two regiments, Tony was going to ensure that his own regiment went out in style. The Regimental History records:

"… *a memorable parade was held in Brooke Barracks to celebrate both Back Badge Day and Imjin Day … As it seemed clear that would be the last major parade in the history of the Gloucestershire Regiment, it was decided to make it an occasion that would be remembered for many a year. Elaborate preparations were made and a large contingent of old comrades flew into Berlin in a chartered aircraft. The 28th/61st marched*

---

[28] The hollow square formation comprises soldiers facing outward along the four sides of a square, with the interior of the square empty.

on in bright sunshine, a light breeze ruffling the colour which was escorted by a full colour guard of seventy-two officers and men. The Commanding Officer, Lt Col HRA Streather, the Second in Command and Adjutant, all mounted and the saluting base was flanked by a guard in the uniform of 1801. The salute was taken by HRH the Duchess of Gloucester ... who fastened the Solma-Ri[29] streamer to the Colour ... The drill was impeccable, RSM Chilcott having been awarded a distinguished grading on his Guards drill course ... and the march-past that followed the trooping was a moving sight. The occasion was recorded by the artist Terence Cuneo who sketched during the parade and subsequently made it a painting that was to hang in the Officers' Mess."

For the next year Tony dutifully complied with the order to amalgamate — that is, until an unforeseen miracle occurred. In the General Election of 1970, Ted Heath's Conservatives beat Harold Wilson's Labour government, and the amalgamation was called off with just twenty-four days to go. Hence at the eleventh hour, the Glosters were reprieved and lived on for a further twenty-four years until the Regiment was finally joined with the Duke of Edinburgh's Royal Regiment in 1994.

In 1969, Tony took the Battalion to Northern Ireland where his quietly effective style calmed the passions of all who dealt with him — his serving officers and not least the Irish community. This was very much a repeat of Cyprus, where he had learned to keep the peace between two warring communities ready for any opportunity to settle old scores.

*1970-73   Chief Instructor of NCO's Wing of the School
                 of Infantry.*

---

[29] Solma-Ri is an alternative Korean name for the Imjin River.

> *Responsible for policy and supervision of all aspects of Skill at Arms training for Officers and NCOs.*
>
> *During this time became Vice Chairman of Army Mountaineering Association and started planning for AMA expeditions to Everest.*
>
> *Organised and led Endeavour Training for young people to the Simien mountains of Ethiopia.*

1973-75   *Returned to Far East in charge of jungle warfare training in Singapore and Malaya. Travelled widely in Southeast Asia studying Communist insurgency.*

Following his command of the 1st Battalion of the Glosters, which he regarded as the highlight of his career, Tony was posted to Warminster as the Chief Instructor of the NCO Wing of the School of Infantry and made responsible for the policy and supervision of all aspects of Skill-at-Arms training for officers and NCOs. This didn't preclude extramural excursions working for Lord Hunt's Endeavour Training scheme. One such expedition involved taking 50 young boys and girls to live it rough in the Simien Mountains in northern Ethiopia. Tony roped in his old friend Philip Horniblow from the AMA Karakoram expedition as expedition doctor, and somehow another old friend, this time from the Kangchenjunga expedition, Joe Brown, was also included. Joe was billed to do some climbing on the highest peak, Ras Dashen, at 14,930 feet but managed to put his back out while demonstrating rock-climbing technique to the awestruck kids. He was invalided out with his wife Val and flown back to the UK for an operation and complete recovery. Further north was the Tigray region, famous for its churches hewn out of solid rock. The authorities were reluctant to reveal their location, but Horniblow recalls Tony offering a small bribe to a local guide and an excited party of teenagers being taken to see a 15th-century church with four portico arches and six internal pillars carved straight out of a mountainside. The expedition was covered by a *Daily Express* man, whose daily reports enthralled readers at home. For the era, early 1970s, it was certainly an exciting and novel experience for everyone involved, especially the youngsters.

1968, Berlin: The Christmas pudding is jointly stirred by the Commanding Officer and the youngest soldier — a time-honoured tradition in the Glosters.

Courtesy of Lt Col (retd) Robert Dixon.

1969, Berlin: The Princess Alice, Duchess of Gloucester, standing in for her husband who was Colonel-in-Chief of the Glosters, taking a final regimental parade before the planned amalgamation with the Royal Hampshires. Commanding officer Lt Col Streather on horseback with sword. The embroidered emblems on the colours (overleaf) list the battles fought by the Glosters, from the 18th century to the present day. In the event, the amalgamation was called off, and the Glosters lived to see another day.

Courtesy of Lt Col (retd) Robert Dixon.

In 1973, Tony left Warminster and returned to the Far East, to the School of Infantry Jungle Warfare Wing, this time based in Johore, Malaysia. This training school had been established in 1948, had its roots in the Burma campaign during the war, but in 1971 had been handed over to the Malaysian Army. Two years later, the School of Infantry realised there was still a need for jungle training and, with the blessing of the Malaysians, co-opted a wing of the school, basing their administrative headquarters just across the Causeway in Singapore. A Commanding Officer and Chief Instructor was sought, and with his previous jungle warfare experience — in the Indian Army and during the Indonesian Confrontation — Tony proved the ideal choice. The assignment lasted two years, until higher authorities decided to close the school down.

A letter written to him by Brigadier Peter Downwood, the Commandant of the School of Infantry, sums up Tony's contribution and shares the frustration of complying with decisions that periodically test a soldier's built-in sense of duty:

"Dear Tony, now that you are back in the country and the Jungle Warfare Wing has been wound up, I would like you to know how very much your sterling work has been appreciated in establishing, running and finally disbanding the unit. There can be no doubt whatsoever that it was a highly successful venture while it lasted and the very high

standard of student you turned out from the course bore testimony to the efficiency and high morale of the unit as a whole. Quite apart from the School of Infantry's point of view in losing such a valuable training establishment, I am deeply sorry that you have had the unenviable task of folding up something which you have put so much personal effort into. I need not mention our own personal feelings on the political issues behind such a move nor what we know will happen in that theatre in the future. For all your efforts as Commandant of the Jungle Warfare Wing and all you have done for the School of Infantry I thank you most sincerely. It would be very remiss of me not to include Sue also in my thanks particularly in the social field and the ever present need to strengthen the good relations with the host countries. Both of you did a most splendid job. Well done." Downwood offers no clue concerning Tony's final and rather cryptic entry for this period: *"Travelled widely in Southeast Asia studying Communist insurgency."* And no clue has ever been forthcoming!

The social side of Tony's posting to Singapore is worth mentioning. Having become firm friends with the Sultan of Brunei previously, he now befriended the Sultan of Johore and through the connection found plenty of opportunity to indulge his passion for polo. The family spent many weekends on board the Jungle Warfare Wing's launch *Beaulieu*, and trips were mounted to the islands off the east coast of Malaysia where Tony passed his jungle skills to the children — lighting fires in torrential rain using tinder from inside fallen trees and building waterproof *bashas*.

By the time Tony and his family returned to the UK, mountaineering was once again taking centre stage. The AMA's plans for Everest had been brewing for five years. It was time for Tony to take charge of his last major Himalayan expedition.

Soldiers on Everest — 1976

The Army Mountaineering Association's ambition on Everest was officially blessed in the Old War Office Building at the Ministry of Defence in October 1971, and planning started soon afterwards. Tony, an obvious choice with unparalleled Himalayan experience, was appointed to take the lead, and he soon pulled in three others: Captain Henry Day, who had been the climbing leader on the AMA expedition to Annapurna the year before and had been the first, with Gerry Owens, to climb the mountain since its first ascent by the French in 1950; Major Jon Fleming who had notched up several expeditions to the Greenland ice shelf; and Major Bob Rutherford whose Edinburgh HQ had sponsored all AMA's expeditions since 1968.

In this era, unlike today, the Nepalese were loath to overload the mountain and each year restricted access to one expedition pre-monsoon and one post-monsoon. Initially, the Army was given a slot for pre-monsoon 1975, but were pipped by a Japanese Ladies' expedition and so were obliged to postpone to 1976. There was some benefit in this because it gave the AMA the opportunity to use 1975 for a Himalayan training climb. The 8,201-metre Cho Oyu was the first choice but ruled out by the Nepalese as too politically sensitive, so it was second-choice Nuptse, the lowest but still very difficult peak in the Everest cirque. By now Jon Fleming had been appointed the leader for both 1975 and 1976 since Tony had been posted overseas to jungle warfare training based in Singapore. The Nuptse expedition was cursed — the summit pair, which comprised Gerry Owens and Richard Summerton from the Annapurna expedition, were lost on the mountain during their assault and another pair of climbers, David Brister and Pasang Tamang, fell to their deaths lower down.

Tony's imminent return to the UK from Singapore at this critical juncture prompted the Army chiefs to rethink the Everest leadership, causing them to favour him rather than Fleming to lead the 1976 expedition. It says a lot for both men that a clearly disappointed Fleming accepted the change, while Tony, although present at the beginning of the planning in 1971 but now parachuted in as leader, managed in his own calm way to gain the respect of all members of the team as they set out for Kathmandu and began the approach march.[30] And it was large group: 29 from the Army, two from the Royal Navy, one from the RAF, three from the Royal Nepalese Army, and a large support team of Sherpas and icefall porters. Somewhere in the mix was Tony's old friend Philip Horniblow, invited to serve as one of the expedition doctors, and Henry Day and Jon Fleming both of whom had been involved in the planning from the very beginning:

Henry Day later wrote up an account of the expedition in the *Himalayan Journal*:[31] *"This was of course a large party but there was a big difference in approach to that of any previous Everest team. Instead of using hired hands to do most of the carrying on the mountain we did this ourselves. We hired only 10 high-altitude Sherpas to work above Advance Base in the Western Cwm and a further 15 icefall porters only 8 of whom actually carried above the lip of the icefall. Our support party of 11 included mail runners and signallers whose high point was Base Camp ... the expedition numbered a total of 73.*

"We walked-in in three main parties almost as soon as we arrived in Kathmandu and took three weeks to Pheriche which was the acclimatisation base. By 6 April the whole team had reached Base Camp.

---

[30] Jon Fleming and Ronald Faux, 1977, *Soldiers on Everest*, Her Majesty's Stationery Office.
[31] Major M W H Day R.E., 1979, *Everest 1976*, Himalayan Journal, vol. 35.

2 Some of the team and reserves outside the wardroom of *HMS Vernon* on 26 January 1976, having been entertained to lunch by HRH the Prince of Wales, patron of the expedition.

1 Major Onslow Dent
2 Sgt. Khagendrabahadur Limbu
3 Captain Philip West
4 Captain Morgan Bridger
5 Captain Brian Martindale
6 Sergeant Roy Francis
7 Major John Muston
8 Mr Ronald Faux
9 Lt. Col. Anthony Streather / Leader
10 Captain Nigel Gifford
11 Lieutenant John Scott
12 Lt. Col. John Peacock
13 Captain Christopher Johnson
14 Flt. Lt. George Armstrong, RAF
15 Captain Terence Thompson, RM
16 Sgt. Christopher Berry
17 Captain Philip Neame
18 Major Henry Day
19 Lt. Col. Richard Hardie
20 Captain Timothy King
21 Captain Patrick Gunson

The Army Mountaineering Association expedition to Everest in 1976 had no shortage of climbers.

Courtesy of the Army Mountaineering Association.

"The ice-fall party of eight strong climbers had occupied Base Camp on 24 March and a camp was placed on 3 April on the block of ice that had been the [Bonington] SW Face team's Camp 1 only a few months before ... Comparing photographs of ours with those taken in the winter, that camp site had descended at least 70 metres. It took another four days' work to make a route through to the Western Cwm. On 6 April, *my party moved up and sited our Camp 1, reaching Advance Base Camp in six hours next day. There was a raised block of ice marked by flags still standing from the winter expedition. The SW Face was black, blown quite clean of any snow."*

1976, Everest: Tony Streather directing operations.
Courtesy of the Army Mountaineering Association.

But tragedy was about to strike, as recounted by Day in a recent communication:[32]

"On 9th April, my birthday, I had roped up with Terry Thompson for the first time. The way into the Western Cwm had been almost opened up by Dick Hardie and the 'Heavy Gang' after prodigious hard work and ingenuity with fixed ropes and ladders. Weaving around the last few long open crevasses we were amazed to find a clearly defined compacted and raised track above an undulating sheet of wind-polished ice. Guided by the raised ribbon of ice there was no problem finding their camp site towards the left side of the cwm. We erected two tents on a flattish section with little levelling needed. There was a large crevasse clearly visible about twenty yards away with a snow bridge across it, which Tony Streather marked. Geordie Armstrong and I shared one tent and Tony Streather another one with Terry Thompson.

"Two days later, Terry and Geordie arrived back after a successful reconnaissance to find a suitable site for Camp 3 at the foot of the Lhotse Face. There was a third tent by now as two Sherpas had joined us as part of the build-up plan. When the time came to retire, I was 'inside man' preparing supper, and Geordie was outside the tent passing in snow to melt and closing things up for the night.

"I heard Tony's voice calling out 'Is Terry over with you?'. It was beginning to get dark so our head torches came out, and Geordie and the Sherpas cautiously searched around. A hole in the surface snow was found; all movement ceased while the lie of the land was inspected as to where was safe. Then Geordie shone a torch and shouted down the hole. It was bottomless but bloodstains were seen — but not Terry.

"I offered to abseil down as I was the slimmest, and also had all the

---

[32] Col M W H Day (retd), 2020, private communication.

gear to hand for descending as well as climbing back up the rope again. After some hesitation Tony agreed that I could try and urged me to be careful. With head torch on, I attached the doubled rope that Geordie had by then tied securely to well-driven snow stakes and squirmed over the lip of the hole which the rope immediately cut into. The displaced snow sparkled in the torchlight and icicles tinkled down.

"*The sides of shiny blue ice initially belled out wider than the rest of the crevasse and I could see what a treacherous trap had been formed. Just Terry's bad luck, he had chosen this spot to stretch his legs. The walls in parts were jagged with icicles, and there were more and more smears of blood. Following them downwards, the crevasse tightened and I was in contact with both walls with no chance of turning around. I could hear groaning now, which seemed to respond to my torchlight.*

"*Terry was on my left, half facing me, upright with his bent legs stopping him falling further. He was uttering loud groans. I spoke quietly and tried to reassure him help was at hand, but I doubt if he knew what was going on.*

"*Another rope had been lowered down by now with a torch on the end so it could be found. I started to try to get the rope around his waist, but it soon became clear it would be better to get a harness onto him that would support his weight with leg loops. It was dark by then and windy up on the surface and Geordie and the Sherpas had difficulty in hearing what I wanted but eventually the harness snaked down. To position the harness around behind Terry I had to get really up close while trying not to hurt him or dazzle him. It was while this was being done that he died.*

"*Eventually the harness was attached and I had done all I could. The strain in the single rope was taken from above by the surface team, amid another shower of icicles, and Terry was lifted slowly up to the surface. I extricated myself from the narrow confines of the ice using ascenders on the double rope, a foot in one loop and a much shorter one clipped to my harness.*

"Next day, Dick Hardie our climbing doctor came up and formally certified that the cause of death had been fatal injuries caused by his fall into the crevasse.

"Throughout all this Tony, who had been through such mountaineering hazards before on K2 and on subsequent expeditions, continued calmly to oversee the rescue, letting each contribute as they were able but ensuring nothing was overlooked. As always, he was a reassuring presence and a great support to all of us." However, as Horniblow relates in his memoir, Tony submitted to being given sleeping tablets that night, he was so upset.[33]

Day's account continues: *"The lowest section of the Lhotse Face proved satisfyingly steep and was well led by Geordie Armstrong. By now we were down to 8 Sherpas and about 20 climbing members. It is pleasant to be able to record that no fewer than 17 members and 6 Sherpas carried loads to the South Col ...*

"A week later we were back on the col as part of Tony Streather's summit plan. There were to be four 'official' summiteers (Brummie Stokes and Bronco Lane; John Scott and Pat Gunson). Camp 6 would be carried up by four climbers (Armstrong, Fleming, Hardie and myself) and the second pair would be supported by Steve Johnson and Phillip Neame. The support climbers could then have a go themselves as circumstances permitted. The logistics were finely calculated ...

"Of course, this was wishful thinking: Everest does not lower her guard for four days on end just when you want it. Camp 6 went in at 8,400 metres on top of the tent left by the Americans in 1963 (empty

---

[33] Philip Horniblow, 2004, *Oil, Sand & Politics: Memoirs of a Middle East Doctor, Mercenary & Mountaineer*, Hayloft Publishing, Kirby Stephen.

cylinders nearby were date-stamped 1962). Brummie and Bronco led the route, being comparatively lightly laden. The top section of the couloir leading to the SE ridge was hard, consisting of steep, deep and insecure snow. There was no security offered by the snow. The going by now was definitely unpleasant. Unconsolidated powder snow lay over rubble and no footstep was firm. Brummie and Bronco both seemed to move in a daze, often making separate tracks although roped together. Visibility by now was very poor; no longer could we see the beautiful pyramid of Makalu nor Lhotse behind us.

"The ridge line by now was corniced and conditions made it difficult to tell where the snow ended and cloud began — one of us could easily have dropped into Tibet while digging out a platform for the tent. I had found the edge of a blue tent showing through an otherwise uniform slope of snow angled at about 40°. Brummie and Bronco had hoped we would carry up to the top of the South Shoulder at 8,500 metres, but I pointed out that the third rope was going very slowly. It was already 2 pm and we had to dig their platform in and get down before dark in obviously worsening weather.

"The loads had been planned in great detail. Brummie and Bronco had packed and were carrying their own rations and personal equipment including the cylinders of oxygen consumed on the way.

"There was an extra rope for the Hillary Step and our lightest radio (0.8 kg). We left them with 6 full tanks of oxygen. In theory they needed 1½ each for the summit and one between them for the night. This left two spare which would be left there for subsequent parties. They also had 24 hours' reserve of rations and fuel.

"I don't remember when the storm began but it was still blowing gale force in the morning … The first radio call was depressing. The assault tent … was not shaping well. Spindrift had filled it through an air vent

now clamped shut with a clip from the oxygen set. Poor night's sleep, morale low.

"I relayed this to Tony at Advance Base using another radio. He had already appreciated the significance of the delay and wanted the first support party down, leaving the second assault group on the col. But as the morning wore on the radio messages from Brummie and Bronco cheered up — they had dug themselves out, the wind was dropping, they hoped to make it next day.

"Throughout the following day, Sunday 16 May, tension mounted. An early morning radio schedule ... established that the summit pair had set off at 6.30 am. The weather was indifferent all day with heavy snow failing in the cwm.

"Bronco and Brummie made good progress up wind-hardened névé to the South Shoulder where they once again met unconsolidated snow. Their account from now on becomes a little hazy. Several hours later they rounded the rock pinnacle on the South Summit ... Photographs they took from there looking upwards show the whole route to the main summit, the Hillary Step having undergone yet another metamorphosis being part rock and part snow with no sign of a chimney. So to the summit where they must have showed great strength of will. For not only did Bronco take photographs with the mandatory pennants, but Brummie read my altimeter and took his heartbeat. The altimeter indicated an increment of 915 metres above the South Col (conventional survey computations indicate 848 metres). Brummie's heartbeat was 98 which sounds impressively low.

"The descent must have been a nightmare. At dusk they found the part-filled oxygen cylinders dumped on the South Shoulder that morning and scraped a little shelter in the lee of the ridge only for the wind to change into their faces. Changing cylinders proved too great an effort so

they shared the last one between them a few breaths each. Somehow they survived the night.

1976, Everest: Brummie Stokes approaching the Hillary Step. Photo taken by Bronco Lane.

Courtesy of the Army Mountaineering Association.

"Meanwhile all camps were again manned and all communications opened ... Regular schedules next morning contained no news and by 9 am, I and I suspect many others feared the worst. The second pair set off prepared for the summit but also to act as a rescue party. At 10 am we heard on the radio that John Scott and Pat had found them frostbitten

and half-dead struggling out of their bivouac site. Dosing them with oxygen they began their laboured descent that was to last five days for one of them.

"We were overjoyed. Tony had tears in his eyes and I think most of us had lumps in our throats — 'That which was lost is found.'

"It took the full team to get them down ... All those who had worked above the col needed a rest down at Base Camp. It would have taken almost two weeks to mount another assault. Many of the members had exhausted themselves carrying on the Lhotse Face, a debilitating activity and perhaps could not be expected to repeat the feat. No one was surprised when Tony announced the inevitable, that the mountain was to be evacuated. So it was over."

Bronco Lane later gave an assessment of Tony's leadership: *"Tony was a senior Officer and spoke Nepalese fluently. He was a very astute man and knew everything that was going on regardless of whether it was a Sherpa or team member. He always used to 'ask' you to do something. He never 'told' you. 'Brummie, will you go and have a look at so and so for me and tell me what you think?' He was calm, collected and had been through it militarily. He understood Nepalese politics, military and the locals very, very well. He put people at ease extremely quickly, always smiling and gave you a gentle bollocking when you needed it! You used to come away agreeing that you needed to improve."*

It was Tony's *Last Blue Mountain*. He could thus add to his achievements: leading a team of men drawn from all three Services to the summit of the highest mountain on Earth. Characteristically, there is scant mention in his CV although it does include mention of an upgrade to OBE:

1976   Returned to UK to take charge of Army Mountaineering Expedition to Everest.

Following successful climb, awarded OBE and elected to follow Field Marshal Templer and Lord Hunt as President of Army Mountaineering Association.

Awarded the Ness award by Royal Geographical Society "for leadership of Army overseas expeditions and other mountaineering achievements."

A Soldier to the End

1976-81 *Posted as Deputy Commandant to Sennelager Training Centre in Germany. Responsible for British Military and some four hundred civilian German staff who administer and run a very large NATO range complex.*

Extramural responsibilities have included being chairman of British Forces Germany Pony Club and Chairman of Local Saddle Club, Polo Club and Game Shoot.

Appointed as a Vice President of Endeavour Training.

Tony's last posting, beginning in 1976, was as Deputy Commandant of the Sennelager Training Centre, controlling a vast area in Northern Germany available for the use of all NATO forces. At the time, it was managed by the British and a large number of so-called 'green men', a workforce recruited at the end of the Second World War from Eastern European refugees. This role did not fit well with a man with such an active background and international fame, and one can see that the subsequent paragraph in the CV talks of more enjoyable pastimes — horses, polo and shooting.

Tony retired from the Army in 1981, and his CV written at this time ends with a modest self-portrait that hints at his unusual career and the reluctance of the Army hierarchy to reward such an unusual man:

> *From the above it can be seen that the bulk of my service has been spent in command or training appointments in many*

> *active service and adventurous parts of the world. My staff experience is minimal, but I have considerable experience of dealing with people of many nationalities under varied conditions. Throughout my service I have taken an active part in extramural activities that have kept me in touch with the civilian world particularly with regard to mountaineering and the training of young people.*

Tony was, above all, a soldier's officer, always there for the individual and willing to bend the rules when it made sense. An example: when commanding the 1st Battalion, he asked why a former National Service officer had turned down an invitation for a regimental reunion. The officer explained that following his return to his civilian life and having held only a National Service commission, he was not permitted to belong to the Officers' Club nor to wear the officers' regimental tie. Tony, incredulous at such pettiness, simply scrapped the rule. The former officer proudly wears the tie to this day.

Similar stories gained widespread currency. On one occasion, a soldier in the Battalion had become bored with routine soldiering whilst on detachment in South Africa. So he signed on as a mercenary with 'Mad Mike Hoare' who was operating a well-paid private army in the Congo. Two years later, on leave from Mad Mike's escapades, he returned to the UK and met a young lady who became his wife. Either her influence or his conscience got the better of him. He reported to the Guard Room at Chester where the Battalion was stationed and gave himself up. He was put on a charge of desertion and faced a court martial. Tony asked to see the soldier's bank statements to verify that he had not surrendered simply because he was hard up — mercenaries were generally well paid. As a result, all charges of desertion were replaced by AWOL (absence without leave), and the man was sentenced to nine months detention at Colchester Correction Centre. Tony had the sentence reduced to six months on review, and the soldier served just three months as an exemplary prisoner. On his return to the Battalion and after a thorough grilling, Tony told him, *"The Regiment can do with men of your experience, but you won't let me down will you?"* The soldier, suitably chastened and reintegrated with his comrades, continued to give loyal and conscientious service to Her Majesty, subsequently became the regimental RSM and was eventually commissioned.

Tony was always anxious to help those whom fate had marked out unfairly. One such was an officer who suffered a crushed leg in an accident and was threatened with an amputation, which for a regular officer meant the end of his career and retirement on a pension of no real worth. The Battalion's Medical Officer, however, had other plans. He suggested to Tony a radical cure that he had once witnessed while practising in Glasgow. This was to have the officer imbibe at least one bottle of whisky a day for a month or more, alcohol being known to dilate the arteries and encourage blood flow to the limb. If this was to work, the problem was hiding a perpetually drunk officer for months on end. Somehow Tony arranged this — the details are murky. The Army authorities never found out, and months later the officer re-emerged sober and cured. He served for many a year afterwards.

One young officer arriving at the Battalion described Tony as a breath of fresh air: *"With his upright manner, neat moustache and clipped quiet voice he was the archetypal commanding officer of the old school. He was not a showman, and he commanded instant respect. In the soldiers' view he was a proper officer and a gentleman."* On one occasion, the young officer was due to go on parade carrying the Colours for the first time. Not being proficient with the drill involved, he was clearly nervous. At that point, he received a message from the Orderly Sergeant: *"Mr Dixon, Sir, the Commanding Officer sends his compliments and would you be so good as to get your arse up to the Officers' Mess immediately"*. With trepidation and fearing the worst, he went post-haste to the Mess to be greeted by Tony, who had a large glass of cherry brandy in his hand: *"I always find a glass of cherry brandy before a big occasion settles things down"*.

Tony being interviewed outside the Officers' Mess at Brooke Barracks, Berlin.
Courtesy of Lt Col (retd) Robert Dixon.

Tony set the highest standards but ensured that he practised what he preached. In Northern Ireland a helicopter was bringing in an officer who was returning to the Battalion and expected to land on the parade ground of the barracks in which the Glosters were housed. However, a drill parade happened to be in progress. The pilot remarked: *"Had I chosen to land on any other barrack square belonging to any other regiment whilst a drill parade was in progress, all those on the ground would have scattered to the sides to avoid the chopper as it came into land — not so the Glosters. Such is the discipline imposed by their CO, I could have landed on top of them and they would not move till told to do so."* The pilot took his passenger to another barracks.

After his official retirement, Tony never really left the Army. His final 'posting', though it was technically not an Army appointment, was as Sports and Estate Manager of the Sandhurst and Camberley estate, housing the Royal Military Academy and Staff College. It was no sinecure. The great storm of October 1987 that swept through southern England caused massive damage to the estate and many beautiful trees were lost. Clearing up the damage fell to Tony and his groundsmen.

The position lasted for ten years and was possibly the longest period that Sue and he spent together in a house of their own. He enjoyed young people, the outdoors job, the tradition of the military training, and the ceremonial parades and attendant parties. And it gave him an opportunity to pass on his wisdom about leadership and courage in adversity. Annually, he would give a series of illustrated talks to Sandhurst cadets of Rowallan Company about his climbing exploits.

As always, horses played a large part in family life. He had two horses bred from an Argentinian polo pony called *Bonnetti* which gave Tony and his daughter Sally many enjoyable hours of riding. Around the estate he would always be seen riding his beloved *Buccaneer*. And the hunting! All those years ago at Fort Sandeman when he had chosen to join the Glosters on the basis that it might provide him some good hunting — now he could finish his career indulging in hunting with the Sandhurst Draghounds as much as he wished, even if it produced the occasional fall and broken collarbone. And though he made little mention of it, the gift by the Sultan of Brunei of money to restore the old Academy Riding School could be traced to Tony's time in Brunei.

Another feature of his life in Sandhurst was keeping a fatherly eye on the foreign cadets, especially those from Pakistan, India and Nepal. On the days of the Sovereign's Parade when the cadets 'pass out' to receive their commissions on completing their courses at Sandhurst, he and Sue would keep open house for the parents of the foreign cadets. The mother of a Pakistan cadet recently remarked that it was so pleasant that Tony could instantly converse in Urdu.

Two Presidents

Tony never enjoyed coping with the bureaucracy that seems to be the lot of those who get elected for office in voluntary associations, yet he became over the years a stalwart President of both the Alpine Club and the Army Mountaineering Association. Tony encouraged both organisations to recruit a younger generation of climbers. In his valedictory address to the Alpine Club, he could honestly remark:[34]

"When you did me the honour of inviting me to become your President, my immediate reaction was that I was much too old and that we should find someone younger. This feeling was prompted by my clear memory of the time when I was first invited to address the Club. It was after the American K2 expedition of 1953 and I was still young and impressionable. There, sitting on those leather benches down the side of the lecture hall at South Audley Street, were the great, the good and the elderly. There was a certain amount of snoring and every now and again there would be a grunt of approval or disapproval depending on what I was saying! This was enough to make any young chap wonder just what he had let himself in for and perhaps it was the image that this created that made it difficult to attract young members in those days."

Tony attended the celebrations in Zermatt of the 125th anniversary of the first ascent of the Matterhorn and in Chamonix the 40th anniversary celebrations of the first ascent of Annapurna. All such occasions kept him in touch with the mountains, which was a blessed relief because most of his two-year term was blighted by the Alpine Club's move out of its Mayfair premises.

---

[34] Tony Streather, *President's Valedictory Address*, read before the Alpine Club on 4 December 1992: Alpine Club Journal, vol. 98: 1-6, 1993.

May 1957: A meet of the Alpine Club at the Pen y Gwryd Hotel celebrating 100 years since the Club's founding. Standing (l-r) G G Macphee, M H Wilson, M H Slater, E N Bowman, C G Wickham, K N Irvine, Sir Arnold Lunn, D G Lambley, L Baume, E J E Mills, H R A Streather*, G F Peaker, H L Stembridge, N E Odell, Sir G Summers, G Winthrop Young*. Seated (l-r) H Westmorland, F H Keenlyside, A D B Side, A K Rawlinson, M H Westmacott*, unknown, H R C Carr, M P Ward, Sir John Hunt*.

A group photo that links many generations of celebrated climbers; an asterisk denotes a President of the Alpine Club.

Alpine Club Photo Library, London.

The Club had leased premises in South Audley Street in the heart of Mayfair at a very small annual rent inclusive of rates. By 1988 the landlord was only too keen to bring this arrangement to an end. Taking advantage of this situation, the Club decided to sell the remaining twenty years of their lease and relocate. George Band, with whom Tony had climbed on Kangchenjunga, assured Tony that all these problems would be resolved by 1990 when Tony was due to follow him as President.

Relocation proved to be a real problem. The plan had been to lease a site from the Royal Geographical Society, but this was opposed by members who felt that the Club's home was somewhere in the mountains and by others who simply didn't like the RGS plan. Tony was parachuted into the middle of these difficulties, and according to all who worked with him, he handled the situation with his usual calmness under pressure, at least on the surface. In the end, new premises were found at Charlotte Road in the City, but not before makeshift accommodations had to be arranged at short notice. As he recounted:

"My two years were dominated by the move and I had little peace from the problems this created. I lost quite a few nights' sleep pondering over the decisions that had to be taken at that time. I hope that, in the long term, they will turn out to have been the right ones ... There was a mass of work to be done in connection with the move and our temporary stay at the Ski Club. The library and our other possessions had to be moved twice, first into store or to the Ski Club and then to our new home. Gangs of willing volunteers, under the able supervision of the indefatigable Bob Lawford, made this possible, while our hard-working Honorary Secretary, Michael Esten, attempted to keep some sort of order in the day-to-day running of the Club. There are too many people to thank them all personally for their help during this turbulent period and, if I tried, I would almost certainly miss some deserving person out; but our thanks go to them all."

The other climbing establishment with which Tony was deeply involved was the Army Mountaineering Association. Having been one of the prime movers at its founding, as described above, he was well positioned to move it forward when he was posted in 1959 to lead the Army Outward Bound School at Tywyn in North Wales. Tony was

President of the AMA from 1992, taking over from Lord Hunt, and remained an Honorary President in perpetuity. On this long journey, he was joined by Honorary Vice-Presidents Sir Chris Bonington and Lt Col John Muston, both also founding members of the AMA, among others. Muston remarked once about expeditioning with Tony: "*One feature of being led by Tony was that, though he seemed to walk rather slowly, he was always one of the first to arrive at the next planned campsite. When gathered round the fire in the evening he would recount his experiences on Haramosh and hold everyone spellbound. There was no emphasis on what he did on that mountain — which was just a plain unvarnished account laced with the lessons that young people could learn from and take away. Even for me, as an old expedition hand, it was a monumental performance.*"

Retirement

At the age of 65 and having worked as Sports and Estate Manager of the Sandhurst and Camberley estate for 10 years, Tony was ready for retirement proper. But a young man called Charlie Rigby had other ideas. Charlie, an ex-Army officer himself, had taken a team of soldiers on a training mission to the snow-capped Hindu Kush mountain range in Pakistan in 1985. He realised that the personal development and camaraderie learned there would shape the team for years to come. In 1988 he decided to set up a company called World Challenge to commercially exploit this notion and in the process created the school expedition industry. The business venture took off, but Rigby decided some climbing gravitas was needed and invited Tony to join as President and Chairman of the Board. As the company expanded from its initial target of private schools to the State sector, World Challenge thrived.

During this period Tony and Sue bought a house, Downside, on the outskirts of the village of Hindon in Wiltshire and then later moved into a smaller house in the High Street known as Apple Tree Cottage. This brought them into the centre of the village and of a thriving community. As a staging post for coaches from London and Dover to the West Country, Hindon once boasted upwards of twelve inns, the archways of which can still be discerned in the houses on the High Street. One of these is *Apple Tree Cottage*. By the time Tony arrived, only two pubs, the Angel and the Lamb remained true to their original purpose, facing each other at the main crossroads in the village. When in the last few months his legs gave him trouble, he would remark as he left the Lamb opposite his cottage on the High Street, *"Once I climbed some of the highest mountains in the world and now I can't manage these bloody steps".*

Having been elected to Honorary Membership of the Alpine Club, he was not finished with the mountains nor with his trusted companions with whom he had climbed them. Every few years there were treks with family and friends to old haunts in Nepal and the North-West Frontier, and team reunions in America and Norway.

At the age of seventy-nine Tony paid his final visit to Kathmandu with Norman Hardie and George Band, for the 50th Anniversary of their ascent of Kangchenjunga. It transpired that he had arranged, with contributions from others, a pension for Dawa Tenzing, the Kangchenjunga sirdar and a special friend to British climbers. The old chap had fallen on hard times. It was not the first time Tony had looked after his well-being. For the AMA Everest expedition, he had ensured that the ageing Sherpa was hired as cook for Advance Base Camp. Tony never forgot anyone who helped him throughout his life and always accorded credit where credit was due.

From Professor Arne Næss, with whom he first learned the craft of high mountain climbing, to his many companions on subsequent expeditions, Tony always projected a rare combination of qualities: a physique that gave him extraordinary aptitude and endurance at high altitude, an undying concern for everyone engaged in the enterprise, be they Hunza porters, Sherpas or his own soldiers, and an innate modesty coupled with a wry sense of humour. At an event organised by the Himalayan Club in Mumbai in 2008, he met Bernadette McDonald, the Canadian author of numerous climbing books. After the meeting, a group of them went for a trek, as she describes:

"We were part of a little group of merry wanderers trekking in the Western Ghats. I recall with such pleasure the late afternoon, post-trail aperitifs on the veranda, where Tony spun tales of adventure that had us

on the edges of our seats. From polo fields at 12,000 feet near the North-West Frontier to leading battalions of soldiers on horseback, disguised as locals to avoid the bullets of snipers, to the summit of Kangchenjunga. His stories spanned the Raj, Partition, the creation of Pakistan, mountaineering victories as well as tragedies and the end of British dominance in Asia.

2005: 50th anniversary of the first ascent of Kangchenjunga in Kathmandu with Norman Hardie and George Band.

Courtesy of the Streather family.

He spoke of a period of history that was colourful, romantic, tragic and cruel. And yet he managed to infuse those intimate stories with such humour that we all wished we had been there with him.

Already in his eighties at the time, his trekking pace had slowed considerably, and the rest stops grew longer as the day progressed, but the impish smile never left his face. It was a rare privilege."

In the Hindon village *Newsletter*, his great friend and fellow churchwarden, Brigadier Geoffrey Curtis wrote:

"Hospitality and integrity are the characteristics of one's thoughts of Tony as the Hindon man. The front door was always open: 'Come in, just the right time for a gin and tonic' ... It was in 1997 that he joined me as my fellow churchwarden. It was a happy relationship and I like to think we were quite a productive team even if there inevitably were those who had other views ...

"Whatever Tony took on, he could be relied upon. The New Year's Day Parties to which all and sundry seemed to be invited were never-to-be-forgotten occasions. I shall always picture him at our house sitting at a table littered with cocktail sticks from his favourite cocktail sausages."

The Reverend Mark Hayter, who officiated at Tony's Thanksgiving Service has the last word:

"When Tony and Sue came to live in Downside, just overlooking the village, over 25 years ago, they quickly established themselves as the most generous of people. One might say, without too much hyperbole, that their generosity was legendary! They were always ready to provide or pay for raffle prizes and suchlike. He would, for instance, always bring a bottle of champagne down to the reception that started the Safari Supper, and send a turkey for the Christmas raffle, and all of these events he frequented with great joy.

"For a number of years, Tony shared the role of churchwarden alongside Geoffrey Curtis, both old soldiers and very near neighbours in the High Street ... It was typical of his care for this place that when his beloved Sue died, in 2005, he should mark her passing with the gift of the glass doors which grace the west end of the church, not only reminding us of her, but also keeping the draught out of the church.

"At every Good Friday service, until his 90th year, he was the one who carried the heavy cross to the altar, just as in his mountains he

would carry the responsibility of getting every last man off the mountain, if he had the strength left.

"Every 31st December, glass of champagne in hand, he would lead his troop up the spiral staircase to the top of the church tower, to see in the New Year. Actually, he himself carried enough bottles and glasses to ensure that the bell ringers and their families all had a celebratory drink.

"While mentioning the bell ringers, he took it on himself to make a 'stay' for the 2nd bell so that it could be rung silently, during practice, by the novice ringers. No mean feat, if you know your bells! This was typical of Tony who took his role seriously, but not with seriousness, and was always the soul of hospitality ...

"Until quite late on, he was regularly seen walking the downs with Keeper, their big, beloved spaniel. The favourite place for a chat would be on his back porch or in the small conservatory at Apple Tree Cottage, where old friends could put the world to rights, and always with the sunniest and readiest smile he would survey the passing village from his front window.

"His devotion to Sue was paramount. He missed Sue sorely. Sue was 'his North, his South, his East, his West'. People such as Tony epitomise the best of the past, so we who are left must be careful with our heritage and ensure it retains the things he cared for and helped to preserve; courage, chivalry, hospitality — in a word, love for his fellow humans.

"Death held no sting for him, as he waited to be reunited with Sue, and perhaps with those whom he had lost on the Blue Mountain and in the years since.

"Goodbye old friend, until we meet again."

Twilight years at Apple Tree Cottage, Hindon, Wiltshire.

Courtesy of the Streather family.

Acknowledgements

Charlie, Peter and Phil Streather and Sally Leech
Lt Col (retd) Martin Bazire
David Boehm
Sir Chris Bonington
Charlie Brown
Col (retd) Meryon Bridges
Brig (retd) Geoffrey Curtis
Richard Davies
Philip Davis
Lt Col (retd) Robert Dixon
Col (retd) Henry Day
Dr Mike Esten
Maj Gen (retd) Robin Grist
Maj Gen (retd) Syed Ali Hamid
Reverend Mark Hayter
Maj (retd) Ivar Hellberg
Gwyneth Horsefield
Glyn Hughes
Mrs Shama Husain
Maj (retd) Tim King
Maj (retd) Alan Ladds
Lt Col (retd) Michael 'Bronco' Lane
Bernadette McDonald
Lt Col (retd) John Muston
Paul Newby
Maj (retd) Claud Rebbeck
Robina Shah

Stephen Venables
Brig (retd) Martin Vine
Richard Vine
Ed Widdick
Anne Wills
The Pakistan High Commissioner, His Excellency Mohammad Nafees Zakaria
The Alpine Club
The Britain-Nepal Society
The Imperial War Museum

BV - #0030 - 150921 - C10 - 198/129/8 - PB - 9781784567804 - Gloss Lamination